The media's watching Vault!
Here's a sampling of our coverage.

"For those hoping to climb the ladder of success, [Vault's] insights are priceless."
– *Money magazine*

"The best place on the web to prepare for a job search."
– *Fortune*

"[Vault guides] make for excellent starting points for job hunters and should be purchased by academic libraries for their career sections [and] university career centers."
– *Library Journal*

"The granddaddy of worker sites."
– *U.S. News and World Report*

"A killer app."
– *New York Times*

One of Forbes' 33 "Favorite Sites"
– *Forbes*

"To get the unvarnished scoop, check out Vault."
– *Smart Money Magazine*

"Vault has a wealth of information about major employers and job-searching strategies as well as comments from workers about their experiences at specific companies."
– *The Washington Post*

"A key reference for those who want to know what it takes to get hired by a law firm and what to expect once they get there."
– *New York Law Journal*

"Vault [provides] the skinny on working conditions at all kinds of companies from current and former employees."
– *USA Today*

VΛULT
> the most trusted name in career information™

VAULT GUIDE TO INTERNATIONAL CAREERS

VAULT GUIDE TO INTERNATIONAL CAREERS

SALLY CHRISTIE
AND THE STAFF OF VAULT

ACKNOWLEDGMENTS

Sallie Christie's acknowledgments: I'd like to thank all the friends, colleagues and classmates who shared their stories and experiences of their time overseas.

Vault's acknowledgments: Thanks to everyone who had a hand in making this book possible, especially Marcy Lerner, Elena Boldeskou and Tyya Turner. We are also extremely grateful to Vault's entire staff for all their help in the editorial, production and marketing processes. Vault also would like to acknowledge the support of our investors, clients, employees, family, and friends. Thank you!

Table of Contents

Visit Vault at www.vault.com for insider company profiles, expert advice,
career message boards, expert resume reviews, the Vault Job Board and more.

VAULT CAREER LIBRARY   ix

Chapter 4: Is an International Career For You? 73

Chapter 5: Practical Considerations 83

GETTING HIRED 91

Chapter 6: Getting Ready 93

Chapter 7: Finding the Job 111

ON THE JOB 141

Chapter 8: What to Expect 143

Visit Vault at **www.vault.com** for insider company profiles, expert advice,
career message boards, expert resume reviews, the Vault Job Board and more.

VAULT CAREER LIBRARY

xi

THE SCOOP

The Benefits of
Working Abroad

CHAPTER 1

A guide to this guide

Welcome to the *Vault Guide to International Careers*. In this book you'll find all you need to know about living and working abroad. Maybe you're already committed to working internationally and have a good idea of where you're going, and what you'll be doing. This book will help you plan properly. Or maybe you bought this book on a whim. This book will introduce you to the possibilities of working abroad. (Please note that this guide assumes that you are North American.)

It's also quite possible that you fall somewhere in between the two groups: you've been thinking about going abroad for a while, but haven't taken any concrete steps yet. Use this book to consider all your options, narrow your choices and get started.

Whatever your situation, this Guide is chock full of ideas on what to do, where to go, and how to do it. Get ready to pack your bags – the world is waiting!

Opportunities aplenty

It's a big world out there: more than 160 countries, 6 billion people, thousands of languages and ethnic groups, and an amazing array of different cultures and religions. Globalization is no longer a buzzword, it is a reality. It is estimated that there are currently 90 million people working outside their country of birth. You could be one of them.

In some countries, such as Australia, working abroad for a year or two after college is extremely common. This is partly due to reciprocal political agreements: Australians under 26 are allowed to work in Commonwealth countries without a work permit. In the United Kingdom, taking off the "gap year," a year off between high school and college, is common.

While the percentage of Americans working internationally has not yet reached the levels of Australia or the United Kingdom, it is estimated that there are 4.1 million Americans (excluding the military) working overseas in a variety of capacities. Of this group, a large number are under the age of 40.

Visit Vault at **www.vault.com** for insider company profiles, expert advice, career message boards, expert resume reviews, the Vault Job Board and more.

V/\ULT CAREER LIBRARY   3

Top Countries for Expatriate Americans

- Mexico – 1,036,300

- Canada – 687,700

- United Kingdom – 224,000

- Germany – 210,880

- Israel – 184,195

- Italy – 168,987

- Philippines – 105,000

- Australia – 102,800

- France – 101,750

- Spain – 94,513

Source: The Association of Americans Resident Overseas

From the desire to see a different part of the world and experience another culture, to seeking a release from domestic boredom, the reasons for going overseas are as varied as the opportunities available and the countries to go to.

The reasons to go

There are five common reasons to go abroad. Most likely, your motivation will combine several reasons.

a. Adventure and personal growth

b. Greater professional opportunities

c. Money

d. Cool resume credentials and long-term career goals

e. Language acquisition

Adventure and Personal Growth

For many, working abroad represents freedom, adventure and the opportunity to break out of the "9 to 5" mold while seeing the rest of the world.

The wealth of experiences you can expect living abroad are far greater than what you might experience at home. When you live outside your home country, your mindset is different, too; you feel an urgency to take advantage of all the opportunities around you that you might not feel at home. Growing up did you only visit famous local sites were when visitors came to town? Well, overseas you're the perennial visitor, and you'll be more likely to take advantage of everything around you.

If you're working in Singapore, for example, flying to the Philippines to scuba dive for the weekend is not just glamorous, it's also feasible. In Brazil, weekends might mean trips into the rainforest with a group of friends. Living in Prague? Go snowboarding on the undiscovered slopes of Eastern Europe.

One year overseas often packs the punch and the memories of five years at home. There is a sense of living life to the fullest in a foreign country, where you experience new situations and adventures almost every moment. Every day, you'll encounter experiences and challenges you wouldn't have to deal with at home.

But not all adventure involves traveling to exotic locales and fabled tourist sites. Experiencing another culture up close and personal can be an adventure in itself. Working and interacting with the local workforce in a professional environment, not to mention actually living in another country, is a rich and rewarding experience.

The first time your Japanese co-worker invites you back to her house for dinner, or the first time you take a bus through the crowded streets of Madrid, will be experiences you will remember forever.

Visit Vault at www.vault.com for insider company profiles, expert advice, career message boards, expert resume reviews, the Vault Job Board and more.

VAULT CAREER LIBRARY

5

Chandra in Saigon

Chandra worked for three years with an advertising agency in Ho Chi Minh City (now often called by its former name of Saigon), Vietnam. After graduating with a degree in marketing from a top university in the United States, she accepted a friend's invitation to visit Vietnam. Initially, she wasn't planning on working there, but after a few weeks in the hustle and bustle of Saigon, she fell in love with the city. She networked locally through her friend's contacts, and soon landed a position as a junior account manager with the local Saigon office of an international advertising agency.

Living and working in Saigon is great, she says, but the best part about the experience is not the job or even the people she's met. It's the weekends. "Sometimes I have to pinch myself," says Chandra, "when I think of the places I've been and the things I've seen. On the weekends we rent motorcycles and explore the jungle. It's cheap, and it's a fantastic way to explore the country. Once we rode to Halong Bay and spent a weekend on the beach where they filmed the movie "Indochine." On long weekends or vacation breaks, all of Asia is at our fingertips. If we have three days off, we might take a train into China, or fly to Bangkok for a couple of hundred dollars.

Sometimes I think of my friends back on Long Island, and the clubs they're going to, and I realize how lucky I am."

Going overseas in many ways is not just a journey to another land, but also a journey inside yourself. Living abroad often leads to greater self-knowledge and awareness. The challenges and frustrations you experience, both in the office and out, will be great drivers of personal growth. Sometimes even the simplest tasks, like getting your phone connected or taking a taxi, put you into situations where you are tested and challenged on a daily basis.

Greater Professional Opportunities

The opportunity for greater professional opportunities is one of the most common reasons cited for going abroad.

In some emerging economies of the developing world, there is often a crucial need for talent. In many economies, qualified personnel are in short supply just at the moment of economic growth when they are most in demand. This is not true everywhere in the developing world, of course, but it is especially marked in some of the fastest growing regions of Asia, Eastern Europe and Latin America. China, for example, is estimated to be growing at a rate of 8 percent a year, compared to barely 2 percent for America last year and even less for some countries in Europe.

While technical skills, such as computer, engineering and medical skills may be most in demand, there is also often a need for Western management experience, even just English language and communication skills. Generally, the less developed the country, the higher the demand for English-speaking expatriates (with the exception of English language teachers).

At home it may seem that every job opening brings with it hundreds of overqualified applicants. By contrast, in many faster-growing areas of the world, there is a dearth of human talent and an educated workforce. Simply having a bachelor's degree from an American university that might not get you a second look at home can be an excellent entrée to jobs bearing more significant responsibilities.

And even if you start off in a relatively junior position, things can change fast. Turnover is greater among expatriates. Many professionals working abroad only do so for a year or two, and when they leave the company can either hire from outside or promote from within. Often, it's promote from within.

There are also greater opportunities to change careers, switch jobs or get involved in something new while working abroad. Breaking into acting and modeling can sometimes be easier overseas than at home. Who knows, you might find yourself on a billboard wearing Golden Dragon brand jeans in Southern China, or dubbing Russian cartoons into English in Moscow.

Sarah in Shanghai

After working for two years with an import/export company in San Francisco, Sarah followed her boyfriend to Shanghai when he was transferred there by his law firm. She networked locally and soon found a job working for a British-based consulting company in Shanghai. The office had just opened when Sarah was hired. At that time, there were only two other staff members.

Once Sarah learned the ropes of the business, she quickly found that speaking English, and being able to interact with the company's mostly foreign client base, gave her an edge over the local employees. The company expanded quickly, and Sarah's responsibilities and position expanded along with it. (It helped that 99 percent of the company's clientele spoke English.)

Within a year, the company had grown from three to 16 employees, and Sarah found herself managing a team of six researchers and delivering on complex consulting projects for multinational clients. The job was not without its challenges, but when evaluating her time in Shanghai, Sarah realizes she most likely would not have had the same experience had she stayed home: "I look at what my friends are doing, working as analysts in banks or at accounting companies, and I realize that my management experience, and the project responsibilities I had by the age of 25 are what a 35-year-old might expect at home."

Economic Incentives

One incentive to go overseas is the chance to find better jobs (or any jobs). Now more than ever, new college graduates often find themselves unemployed and with limited prospects at graduation. It has been estimated that the downturn in the United States economy between 2001 and 2003 resulted in up to 50 percent fewer job opportunities for college graduates. In this environment, moving overseas into an area of the world that is still experiencing economic growth can be a smart career move – and a way to ride out the economic downturn.

College placement personnel encourage the move. Says one career counselor from Columbia University: "We've seen an increase in the number of students looking to work abroad after graduation, mostly in teaching. This is a great way to start working and start getting a handle on their student loans when jobs here are hard to come by."

Some practical considerations make an international job search quite feasible (depending on location.) Living abroad, especially in developing countries, can be cheaper than living in America.   For example, launching a job search and surviving for a few months off credit card debt is easier if you are looking for a job in Krakow, Poland, than in New York. Both are major cities with good opportunities, but the budget for a three-month job hunt in Krakow looks very different from the same one in New York. There are, however, some major cities where the cost of living exceeds that of most American cities; Tokyo and London can be extremely expensive places to live while searching for jobs. Choose your target accordingly.

Adventure

Just as many people go abroad to escape unpleasant economic realities, many also go to escape harsh "motivation realities." Going abroad can be a way to explore what you want to do with your life.

Don't know what you want to do after graduation? Joining a big company doesn't appeal to you? You've got an English degree and have no idea what to do next? If you don't know what to do with your life, perhaps you should hit the road.

However, don't use an international excursion as a panacea for the employment blues. If your only motivation is push (escape) rather than pull (for example, the desire to experience another culture), you may not last long. Working overseas can be physically and emotionally challenging, and your heart really has to be in it to survive. As the director of international programs at a Midwestern university notes: "I would not recommend looking for work abroad as a substitute for finding a job at home, if simply having a job is the main goal. Go primarily for the experience of living abroad, to be immersed in a different culture."

Money

Working abroad can be more lucrative than working domestically – but not always. But it's safe to say that going global can be more profitable than staying home. This is especially true for professionals who are transferred overseas by their companies. In these cases, the company often gives relocated employees a generous "expat package," paying expenses such as relocation, airfare, housing, and generous vacation allowances.   Some companies even take care of an employee's taxes during their time abroad.

Visit Vault at **www.vault.com** for insider company profiles, expert advice, career message boards, expert resume reviews, the Vault Job Board and more.

VAULT CAREER LIBRARY

9

But even if your company doesn't transfer you, working overseas can nonetheless be very lucrative. Salaries in many jobs are higher, and promotions come quicker, enabling you to earn more money in jobs with more responsibilities than you would back home.

Often, however, the greatest difference comes on the cost side of the equation: While your salary may be the same or lower than you would have earned in your home country, your expenses may be significantly lower. This is especially true if you are targeting a country outside Europe or Japan. In many developing countries, the cost of living, including such necessities as rent and food, is a fraction of the cost of living in North America. This allows you to save more.

The technical term for this is "purchasing power" – the comparison of what a similar dollar amount would buy in various countries. For example, $10 will get you a movie ticket in New York City, but for the same amount of money in Sao Paolo, Brazil, you could see a movie AND buy two beers AND eat a steak dinner.

Note that these cost savings only apply if you are prepared to adopt a "local" lifestyle. In every major city around the world, no matter how cheap the local cost of living is, there exists housing targeted at foreigners on company expense accounts. These "foreigner apartments" rent for many times more than "local" housing. There are also bars, restaurants and entertainments that cater to foreigners – company expats and tourists. Prices are often the equivalent of what you'd pay in your hometown. So, if you are truly interested in saving money (and having a more rewarding cultural experience) live as much like the local inhabitants as possible.

Escaping a Lousy Economy: Jared in Indonesia

Jared graduated from college in the early 1990s into one of the worst recessions of the century. With no immediate job prospects, he decided to go to Indonesia a few months after graduation. A friend of his from high school had graduated the previous year and was living and working in Jakarta. This friend offered Jared a place to stay while looking for work, and assured him that finding work teaching English would be a snap.

Having a friend who offered to support him for a few months was a major motivating factor in deciding to move to Jakarta. Once there,

Jared found a job within a few weeks working at a leading Jakarta business English school. The money wasn't terrific, but life in Jakarta was so cheap that he was still able to save some money every month.

While teaching, Jared was able to meet a cross-section of Indonesians, and made many friends and valuable contacts. "Contrary to what I'd been told, my students were all really friendly and very interested in getting to know me outside of class. I was invited to several homes, and on holidays and weekends I often went on excursions with my students and ex-students."

Through one of his classes, Jared met an Indonesian businessman. Jared and he initially became friendly when he asked for Jared's help with proofing legal documents. They got to know each other better, and a few months later he approached Jared to join a new company he was setting up in the timber business. "I obviously didn't have any experience in wood – does anyone, really? – but he recognized that having an American on staff would serve as a valuable liaison with the U.S. market and our potential clients."

Years later, Jared is still in Indonesia. The new company is thriving, exporting timber products back to a variety of end-user businesses in the United States. Because of his language skills and the small size of the company, Jared has had responsibilities in many areas: marketing, sales, logistics and finance. He says he can't imagine what he would be doing if he were still back home in Chicago. "Working at Starbucks?" he speculates.

Visit Vault at **www.vault.com** for insider company profiles, expert advice,
career message boards, expert resume reviews, the Vault Job Board and more.

V/\ULT CAREER LIBRARY

11

Shawn in Shanghai

Shawn, 28, makes about $10 an hour as an English teacher in China at a private kindergarten. He shares an apartment near the center of the city of Shanghai with two other teachers and pays $300 for his portion of the rent. They live in "local" housing, in an apartment complex inhabited mostly by middle class Chinese. He only spends about $200 on eating and drinking per month, and finds that, with the private tutoring he does in addition to his main job, he can easily save $1,000 every month.

"$10 an hour may not sound like a lot, and in fact it's a lot less than I was earning back in Ohio, but with low taxes and the incredibly cheap cost of living in Shanghai, I feel like I'm living like a king and saving money at the same time!

For example, eating lunch at one of the little restaurants near the school is only 80 cents. Dinner out with friends at local restaurants is never more than $5, no matter how much food or beer we order! Going to the movies is only $2, not to mention just released bootleg DVDs on the street for $1. Last weekend we took a trip to a local island. A bus ticket to the coast was 35 cents, and then the two-hour ferry ride cost a whopping $3! The whole weekend probably cost us no more than $15 each."

Cost of Living Survey

Interested in knowing which cities are more expensive than others? Every year Mercer Human Resource Consulting does a Cost of Living Survey. For 144 countries, Mercer compares the price of goods, including housing, food, clothing and household goods.

One note: This survey focuses on a "standard shopping basket for any expatriate assignment," meaning they are focused on high-end rent and shopping in foreign supermarkets for (mostly) foreign goods. If you're planning on living in more local style, some of the Top 10 would change: Beijing and Seoul, for example, are definitely not going to be more expensive than New York, but Tokyo and Geneva would still remain high on the list.

The Top 10

1. Tokyo, Japan

2. Moscow, Russia

3. Osaka, Japan

4. Hong Kong

5. Beijing, China

6. Geneva, Switzerland

7. London, UK

8. Seoul, South Korea

9. Zurich, Switzerland

10. New York City

Resume Credentials and Long-Term Career Goals

The enhanced responsibilities and the challenges that often come from working internationally can be a great way to differentiate yourself and add luster to your resume. International experience can give you an edge when applying to graduate school, or help provide the foundation for a long-term international career.

Regardless of the industry or job that you are in, working overseas helps demonstrate that you have the flexibility and adaptability necessary to thrive in another culture. Flexibility, international sophistication and sheer grit are highly valued by many graduate programs, especially by law and MBA schools.

What type of international experience is most valued? Says one admissions officer from the Wharton MBA program: "Having international experience is always a plus, if the candidate pursues that option by choice. Doing something unexceptional abroad just [to get international experience] on a

Visit Vault at **www.vault.com** for insider company profiles, expert advice, career message boards, expert resume reviews, the Vault Job Board and more.

V/\ULT CAREER LIBRARY   13

resume is not compelling to the (admissions) committee. International experience is helpful since it provides an incoming student perspectives that will help them adjust to an extraordinarily diverse community. To understand people and ideas from multiple perspectives greatly increases a student's ability to benefit and contribute at a higher level while they are attending Wharton, as well as after they gradate in their jobs, relationships and communities."

Kelly in Russia

Kelly, 25, applied to Columbia Law School in her senior year of college. When she wasn't accepted, she decided to go to Russia. She had always had a vague interest in living overseas, and a Russian language course had piqued her interest in the country. She initially studied Russian for a semester, and then decided to work while continuing to study part-time. She eventually found a job working in Moscow with an international moving company, helping foreign businesses set up shop in Russia.

The experience gave her significant insight into the legal aspects (and problems!) of doing business in a foreign country. When she reapplied to Columbia two years later, she was able to leverage her business and legal experiences in her application essays and was admitted.

Language Acquisition

Sometimes, the primary motivation to spend time overseas is the chance to learn another language, or improve upon one you've already studied. Fluency in another language opens doors to many types of careers, including international business, the diplomatic corps, trade, teaching and tourism. Fluency alone won't guarantee a job, but as a supplement to other skills the knowledge of a foreign language is undeniably valuable. The fastest, most effective way to learn a language is to actually live in the country and immerse oneself in the culture.

You may have already studied a second language in high school or college, but be prepared: Even four years of university text books and conversation classes won't necessarily prepare you for the living language. You might find yourself unable to read a menu or order a cup of coffee.

If you want to learn a second language, but have no background in any particular one, which should you choose? If you're looking long term to your future, pick a language that will be in strong demand in multiple parts of the world. English is of course a truly global language, but there are a host of other languages that are equally important in the trade and business of their region. Russian is the lingua franca of the ex-Soviet Union states. French is a common language in West Africa, and Arabic in the Middle East (though be wary of dialects). Mandarin Chinese is used in many parts of Asia. Spanish is widely spoken in Central and South America. The language spoken by the most native speakers after English? Hindi.

Some languages are easier to learn than others. Count on two years of full-time study before being able to conduct business in Chinese, but six months of living and working in Ecuador would probably get you up to speed in Spanish.

If you choose to formally study a language, there are a number of different options available. You can study at a university, as part of a language exchange, or at private institute. Programs and courses can either be full-time or part-time. Full-time, of course, is going to be more expensive than part-time, but depending on the country and situation, you may be able to pick up enough side work (for example teaching English) that will leave you with a flexible schedule and enough money to support your language "habit."

Visit Vault at **www.vault.com** for insider company profiles, expert advice, career message boards, expert resume reviews, the Vault Job Board and more.

V∧ULT CAREER LIBRARY

15

Learning through doing?

Of course, you can always learn the language of the country you're working in without taking classes. By being immersed in the local culture, you'll naturally pick up some of the language, and with some extra effort (and some innate ability) you may become fluent by yourself. If you think of yourself as surrounded by teachers-cum-local residents, you will find many people that are more than happy to help you. Try a language exchange: Find a local friend who wants to learn English, and exchange lessons with each other.

But even if you're living in the country, you still have to make an effort. You will not learn a language fluently by "osmosis." You will probably pick up enough to get by, but you'll rarely become truly fluent unless you make an effort. This is especially true in countries where the language is not remotely related to English. Don't expect to learn Korean or Swahili unless you really apply yourself!

Finally, if you're serious about language acquisition, don't let your lifestyle sabotage you. While it's natural to gravitate toward fellow English-speaking expats and locals, make sure you spend time speaking the language outside the classroom with native speakers.

Opportunities Abroad

CHAPTER 2

What can you do?

So you've decided that you'd like to work overseas. Now, we'll explore some of your job options.

In almost every country, you'll find an interesting mix of foreigners who, for a variety of reasons, are now working and residing abroad. These sojourners range from "expats" working for multinational companies, to English teachers, to students studying the local language, freelance writers, missionaries, development workers, diplomatic workers and entrepreneurs. There's also often a cadre of young foreigners in "professional services" – working for companies that target the rest of the foreign community, or in local companies where a Western background is often the primary consideration for the job.

Vault has identified eight common types of international workers:

a. Corporate Transfers

b. "Half-Pats"

c. English Teachers

d. Foreign Service Officers

e. Development Workers

f. Entrepreneurs

g. Temporary and Seasonal Workers

h. Students

Of course, this is just a sampling of the types of expatriates you'll find in any large city overseas. Included in this eclectic mix would also be traders, journalists, lawyers, doctors, missionaries, military, and many others.

Visit Vault at **www.vault.com** for insider company profiles, expert advice, career message boards, expert resume reviews, the Vault Job Board and more.

V/\ULT CAREER LIBRARY

17

Corporate Transfers

Who they are

The vast majority of the companies in the Fortune 1000 have operations outside continental North America. And as large companies set up international shops, they often transfer employees abroad.

The cost of sending an employee overseas is significant. Professionals transferred by their companies often have generous "expat packages" that take care of housing, relocation, schooling, and offer perks such as extra salary and bonus, "hardship" pay, and extended vacation time. The days of the full-fledged expat are numbered from the start, however: Once local employees have been sufficiently trained, the position is often "localized" with a local hired to do the same job (typically at a fraction of the cost to the company). A local employee, once trained and developed sufficiently, will take on the role once the "knowledge transfer" is complete.

In addition to knowledge transfer, another type of transfer is important to global companies. This is "culture transfer" – disseminating the corporate culture to distant offices. Culture transfer is often achieved through routine rotations of workers between offices. In many of these companies, an overseas stint is expected, and can sometimes be crucial for advancement within the company.

Qualifications

The surest way to land an expat assignment is to join a company with a global presence that regularly sends junior and mid-level employees overseas. Many multinational corporations (MNCs), fit this bill. By definition, a multinational is a company with offices outside of its home country. All large multinationals, whether they specialize in consumer goods, industrial production, financial services or consulting, have offices and production all over the world, and many offer international rotations to their employees as a perk – or a necessity.

Some industries, such as shipping and energy, are more global than others. While they are not among the "sexiest" of industries, joining one of these industries virtually guarantees you a global career. For example, Maersk, one of the largest shipping companies in the world, offers a two-year management trainee program that hires more than 400 young college grads from 80 countries every year, grooming them for a global career within the shipping and logistics industry.

MNCs in other industries are also known for their global orientation. In these companies, including household names like Citigroup and General Mills, an international stint is virtually guaranteed to anyone interested. Many offer two-year management and associate trainee programs that include international rotations.

If you're not in a rotational program, don't expect to be transferred by your company until you've worked with them for a while. Most large U.S.-based corporations will not hire young employees or recent grads for overseas assignments. The exception may be if you have existing work authorization or special language skills.

So – the bottom line is if you're committed to an international career and would like to work abroad under the aegis of a large corporation, find a company that will rotate you overseas shortly after joining them, or be prepared to spend a significant amount of time working your way up the ladder. Otherwise, don't expect to be transferred immediately to an overseas office.

Uppers and downers

The size of your company and the frequency with which employees are transferred between offices will help determine how seamless the transfer is,

International Trainee Programs

Most of the international management rotation programs are found at the post-graduate (law, MBA, or other graduate degree) level, but a few are also for entry-level graduates. Many other companies will offer international assignments on a more informal level to their employees

Citigroup: One of the largest multinationals in the world, and the most global bank, with operations in 97 countries. Citigroup boasts a number of management trainee programs, many of which include an international rotation: Check out their Finance, HR and Support & Logistics Programs. The GEMMA (Global Emerging Markets Management Associate) program, a two-year global rotation program for new MBAs, is currently suspended due to re-organization. www.citigroup.com

Cargill: Cargill is one of the largest agribusiness companies in the world. Cargill has a post-grad two-year management trainee program called the Strategy and Business Development Program (SBD). Cargill is based in Minneapolis; participants work on projects around the world and are later transferred to global business units. www.cargill.com

Colgate-Palmolive: This consumer products powerhouse's Global Marketing Program and Global HR Program both include international rotations for post-grads. www.colgate.com

General Electric: Has a number of management and leadership development programs. While an overseas rotation is not guaranteed, the global nature of many of GE's businesses means many opportunities to get involved in international projects and work with other countries. www.ge.com

McGraw Hill: Publishing is a global business. Check out McGraw Hill's highly selective two-year ADP (associate development program); a rotation outside the U.S. is guaranteed for one of your three assignments during the 24 months. www.mcgrawhill.com

Merrill Lynch: Like many global banks, Merrill places strong emphasis on global hiring. The company hires graduates into a variety of core areas, with international placements possible. www.ml.com

and what is taken care of for you, and what is not. Some offices, for example, will have moving companies they work with closely who take care of all their relocating employees. Other companies might just provide you a stipend for moving expenses, and expect you to do the rest of the work.

Going overseas as a corporate transfer is usually very lucrative. It can also be a good career move in many global companies (though it isn't always – out of sight means out of mind in some "home country" offices.) Finally, you'll remain with a company that's familiar to you, which can mean a lot in a strange environment.

Lingo

Dipkids: Children of diplomats, found in major cities all over the world.

Expat: An expatriate is simply someone living outside his or her country of origin, but in the corporate world "expat" has a different connotation. Usually, this shortened version of expatriate refers to a senior corporate transfer on a "full expat package" (see below).

Expat scene: The social scene in any major city where expats and their families congregate. The expat scene could be centered around a sports club for foreigners, or around various nationality-driven associations. Students and teachers aren't usually part of the "expat scene."

Full expat package: The salary and perks that an "expat" gets. Quite attractive when relocation, schooling, housing, vacation, tax breaks, training, etc, are taken into account.

Going local: A term used by foreigners to refer to other foreigners who have adopted the local lifestyle and culture.

Hardship allowance: Additional monetary allowance provided for individuals and families living in "hardship" posts: i.e. those places where some of the basic western necessities of life can't be found.

Halfpats: Foreigners not on the "full expat package." Usually hired locally, or at a more junior level. See the next section for more details.

Local hire: In certain contexts, refers to a foreigner hired in-country (i.e. locally) for a position. Local hires, unless they are very senior, don't usually receive the "full expat package."

Localization: Refers to the practice of transforming an expat position into one filled by local nationals. For example, an expat may be hired to run a factory in China, on the understanding that at the end of the five-year term, he will have trained his replacement and the position will then become 'localized'.

Visit Vault at **www.vault.com** for insider company profiles, expert advice, career message boards, expert resume reviews, the Vault Job Board and more.

VAULT CAREER LIBRARY   21

The "Half Pat"

Who they are

The "half pat" is the corporate transfer's poorer cousin. The term "half pat" was coined to describe those foreigners living and working abroad who were not transferred by their companies, and hence not on full "expat packages." Half pats are said to earn about half of what their richer expat cousins earn, hence the name. Of course, this is not always true, but it's a useful way of distinguishing the two groups.

Local companies wanting to hire foreigners will often look for foreigners who are already in country. In this way they avoid relocation costs, thus saving themselves much of the costs incurred in a corporate transfer. Big multinationals and other foreign companies will also hire foreigners "on the ground." If hired in country (especially for more junior positions) you should not expect to receive all the perks and salary you might have had you been a corporate transfer.

Half-pats are often younger and more inexperienced than the typical corporate transfer. They can be found working in areas where their English and Western communication skills are indispensable, often in professional service industries that cater to the more affluent expat population.

Potential half pat functions might include:

• Professional services and all types of consulting

• Moving and relocation companies

• Shipping

• Import/export companies

• Human resources

• Real estate

• Sales and marketing

• Hospitality and tourism

Often speaking English is enough to get hired as a half pat. Knowing the local language is always an asset, but it is not always essential. One recent study looking at hiring qualifications for overseas positions noted relevant job experience, technical skills and the ability to function well in a foreign culture as the top requirements. Rated as less important were "good awareness of cultural issues" and, perhaps surprisingly, the ability to speak a foreign language. (The lower priority assigned to linguistic skills is most likely due to the fact that English is the international language of business.)

Countries where native language skills are less important include China, Vietnam, Indonesia, and smaller countries such as Cambodia. Professionals in certain European countries, such as Germany, Scandinavia and the Netherlands already speak English fluently, so English skills are not much of an asset – but then again, the lack of the native language isn't as much of a hindrance.

In South America, where Spanish and Portuguese are the languages of business, you will need to know the language to be hired for most jobs. In emerging markets in Eastern Europe, locals will likely learn Russian before English as their second language, so a knowledge of Russian is useful when working on a professional basis.

So do you need to know the local language? It depends to a great extent on:

- **Who your main clients are:** If you're interacting on a daily basis with an end clientele who is English speaking, then knowing the local language won't be as important.

- **The level of English knowledge in the country:** As mentioned above, in many areas of Europe much of the professional population is already fluently bilingual. In many areas of Eastern and Southern Africa, English is the lingua franca of business. English is an official language in India.

- **Your level of seniority:** The more senior you are, the less important language acquisition is. You'll be hired for your technical skills, not for your communication ability.

Qualifications

Typically, half pats are less advanced in their careers and have more general skills. A university degree is often their only formal qualification for a position.

Half pats are generally not hired from abroad or through typical career recruiting channels, but most are hired "in-country." If you want a job working for a building developer in Cambodia, or a medical evacuation company in Brazil, you're going to have to show up, start pounding the pavement and networking.

Visit Vault at **www.vault.com** for insider company profiles, expert advice, career message boards, expert resume reviews, the Vault Job Board and more.

VAULT CAREER LIBRARY   **23**

Uppers and downers

This type of work offers a quick way to work internationally in a professional capacity. It helps if you're not wedded to one particular area or industry, and can go where the opportunities are greatest and be flexible in your choice of jobs.

Expect a grittier work environment and more unpredictability in the workplace – despite the reputation or establishment of the company overseas, smaller branch offices of companies often look very different than the offices in the home country.

Patrick in Beijing

Patrick went to Beijing after graduating from college with a degree in East Asian Studies. He wasn't sure exactly what he wanted to do with his degree, but realized when he got to China that there was a tremendous amount of opportunity. While living with an expat friend in Beijing working for a multinational, Patrick networked among the foreign population, and quickly landed a job with a real estate company. "I had thought that not speaking Mandarin fluently would be a major hindrance," he says, "but when I arrived in China I realized that speaking English, and being a Westerner, was probably more important for many jobs than speaking Chinese."

This is not true for all jobs in China, of course, but at the real estate company the primary clients were foreigners relocating to China for business. Therefore, the language of communication was English. Patrick says: "There were very few Chinese working in my particular department, because we dealt with foreign clients, and generally clients like to deal with salespeople who can speak their language. A lot of my co-workers were like me – they had little experience in China and didn't speak Chinese. We were hired mainly for our sales ability and our ability to network with the foreign population."

Patrick started off in residential sales, then moved to commercial real estate. He now works primarily with American companies looking to lease office space in Beijing. "The work is fascinating and gives a great overview of the changes going on within the economy – I can see what type of companies are coming, and who is leaving. And it's amazing to be a part of such a fast-growing economy."

The English Teacher

What is it?

Teaching English as a Second Language (ESL) has evolved into a global industry. Teaching English abroad has become a great way to spend a few years overseas and experience the world before returning home. From Japan to Bulgaria, from Swaziland to Brazil, you will find a market for ESL almost anywhere.

For workers in many countries, fluency in English is a ticket into the best high schools and universities, as well as into the global economy. Which helps explain why every day, with classes starting as early as 6 a.m. and continuing through to 10 p.m., millions and millions of students all over the world attend English classes. And they all need teachers to help them do it.

The World of English Teaching Acronyms

TOEFL: Test of English as a Foreign Language (English proficiency test)

TESL: Teacher of English as a Second Language

TEFL: Teacher of English as a Foreign Language (same as above, but more common in the U.K.)

ELT: English Language Teacher

ESL: English as a Second Language

So, what does "teaching English" mean? The job can cover a wide variety of tasks and situations. You may find yourself chatting with students in a "conversation class," teaching grammar and writing, or helping students prep for high school exams, the TOEFL and the SAT. A common situation is teaching at a "language institute" set up solely for the purpose of teaching English. Students come to these institutes for an hour or two every day, taking courses lasting from a few weeks to several months. As a teacher at one of these institutes, you might be teaching up to eight classes a day, often split between early morning classes and late afternoon/evening classes.

In addition, English teachers can be found working in private kindergartens, elementary and high schools, in the public education system, in government-

Visit Vault at **www.vault.com** for insider company profiles, expert advice, career message boards, expert resume reviews, the Vault Job Board and more.

V/\ULT CAREER LIBRARY

25

run programs, in company training programs, volunteering in remote villages, working at prestigious universities and on remote oil rigs. Some of these positions require more teaching qualifications and experience than others. The fact that a teacher is a native speaker of English is the most important qualification for the job.

Because of the diversity of experiences, the flexibility of requirements and the low barriers to entry, teaching English attracts a wide variety of people, from career professional ESL teachers with Master's degrees, to (more commonly) younger teachers in their 20s and 30s.

The two most common areas of the world to teach English in are currently North Asia (Korea, Japan, China, Taiwan) and Eastern Europe (the Czech Republic, Poland, and countries like Bulgaria and Hungary). As it prepares for E.U. admission, Turkey has also seen increased demand for English teachers. Latin America also offers some opportunities, though here the demand for "native speakers" is not as high and many language courses rely on locals with good language skills.

So, where should you go? It depends on your motivation for wanting to teach English in the first place. Is it lifestyle or money that is motivating you? Are you interested in a certain part of the world?

If you're interested in money, there are places where teaching can be quite lucrative. North Asia is still your best bet if making and saving money is your goal. Private tutoring (teaching private or small group lessons on the side) provides ample opportunities to make extra money. Hourly rates can range up to $50/hour, though the best gigs are often monopolized by teachers who have been in the country for a long time.

China currently does not offer salaries that match with those offered in Japan, Korea or Taiwan, though demand for private lessons and English teachers is increasing as the economy there expands. Teaching English in certain Middle Eastern countries, such as Dubai and Saudi Arabia, can also be lucrative, though these positions are typically limited to men for cultural reasons.

In other areas of the world, the attraction of teaching English is less about the money. As the director of an ESL institute in Prague says: "We provide accommodation assistance, pay work permit and residency visa fees, pay for health insurance and teacher bonuses. However, if you are hoping to put aside money to pay off student or housing loans in your home country, you should consider teaching elsewhere. Above all else, you should come to Prague for the experience."

Qualifications

One of the main attractions of teaching English is the abundance of positions available and the ease with which you can get a job. For many positions, the only requirement is an undergraduate degree (an English or education degree is usually preferred but not required) and possibly a TEFL (Teacher of English as a Foreign Language) certificate. TEFL certificates can be obtained in as little as four weeks (100 to 120 classroom hours) from a growing number of centers around the country and globally. You can take the courses in practically any location in the world.

What do you learn during the TEFL certificate course? You learn the basics of teaching techniques and material development, the fundamentals of grammar and writing, and how to motivate and involve students. You'll get lesson plan ideas. In some cases the programs put you through a foreign language course so you can have the experience of being a language student yourself. Unless you're taking the course online, there will also be a "Teacher Practice" component, which teaches you to run a class in a real setting.

There are hundreds of accredited schools that offer the TEFL. Most courses are affiliated with local language institutes and potential teaching positions, so taking the course in situ is a good way to scope out jobs and make contact with potential employers. Once you have your certificate, you can either accept a job in the country of study, or go elsewhere – the certificate is good all over the world.

Another option is to take the TEFL course online. This is often a cheaper option, and allows you to take the course part-time while continuing your day job. The main downside of taking the course online is that you miss out on the Teacher Practice component of the classroom certificate.

The cost of the certificate ranges from a few hundred dollars for the online option to a few thousand dollars on site, if meals and accommodation are included.

Other than your BA and a TELF certificate, what else makes a successful teacher? There is no one formula, but it's safe to say that a certain amount of confidence is necessary, as well as creativity, flexibility and a genuine interest in helping others succeed.

Uppers and downers

Perhaps more than any other job you might take overseas, teaching can get you closer to the local population and give you insights into the culture.

Visit Vault at **www.vault.com** for insider company profiles, expert advice, career message boards, expert resume reviews, the Vault Job Board and more.

VAULT CAREER LIBRARY   27

"Teaching English in Tokyo was a wonderful way to learn about Japanese culture," says Robin, who taught English for three years in Japan. "When I wanted to know how Japanese viewed, for example, the issue of intermarriage, I simply made it into that night's conversation topic!"

While some make teaching English a career (and for those so inclined, there are advanced degrees available), for many teaching English is a way to spend a few years earning money and exploring the world. Where the "typical" English teacher goes next is hard to say. Many teachers learn the language and move into professional positions in the country where they taught. Others manage schools or open their own schools. Still others return to grad school or jobs back home.

But regardless of what you might consider doing post-teaching, teaching ESL can help you develop some valuable skills. These include public speaking, presentation and communication skills, facilitation skills, creativity, and a deep understanding of another culture.

Despite the numbers of young people teaching English, the seemingly never-ending demand, and the relative ease with which you can get a job, teaching English is not all a bed of roses. Much depends, of course, on the situation you find yourself in, but some of the drawbacks include:

- **Disreputable institutions:** Not all English schools are on the level. One of the major risks of teaching English abroad is shady institutes overworking and ripping off teachers, and in some cases causing visa and legal problems.

- **Inadequate resources and training:** Some teachers must begin to teach less than 24 hours after arrival, with no teaching experience or training. Others complain about shoddy lesson plans, no textbooks and the need to create all their materials from scratch.

- **Split shifts and hectic schedules:** If you're working for a private institution, you may experience a "split schedule," with classes starting as early as 6 a.m. and finishing as late as 10 p.m. The classes offered by these types of institutes often cater to working professionals, and schedule the classes both before and after work for their convenience. For the teacher, it means a long day – albeit with a break of several hours in the afternoon

Foreign Service Officers

Who they are

The Foreign Service is often the first thing that comes to mind when people think of a global career. And unlike many of the other opportunities covered in this book, a Foreign Service career is indeed that – a career. Joining the Foreign Service means accepting a professional (and personal) life spent overseas, with constant rotations every few years. It can be very rewarding, exciting and occasionally glamorous work.

While the salary generally does not match what you can make in the private sector, generous allowance perks and subsidies help make up the difference. For example, there is a hardship "bonus" for postings in difficult areas of the world, up to 25 percent above your base salary. One Foreign Service Officer commented on the pay: "There's a lot of internal grumbling about the salary, but it's really not that bad. When you look at the remuneration, you have to look at the whole package, including subsidized housing and unlimited access to American military exchanges and the American-priced foodstuffs."

Applicants enter the Foreign Service in one of five career tracks: Management Affairs, Consular Affairs, Economic Affairs, Political Affairs and Public Diplomacy. Which career track you enter as a beginning FSO (Foreign Service Officer) will influence the nature of your assignments and your career, and there is little crossover between the tracks once you have made your decision. FSOs often undergo intensive training before being posted to their first overseas assignment, including, in some cases, up to two years full-time language study. Check out www.state.gov for more information on the application procedure, and also www.afsa.org, the American Foreign Service Organization, for more information on what life is like in the Foreign Service.

Qualifications

While potential FSOs come from all backgrounds, being accepted is extremely competitive – roughly 40,000 applicants apply for the Foreign Service exam every year, only about 400 are eventually accepted. If you are serious about joining the Foreign Service, be prepared to do your homework!

The exam is offered once a year, and studying for it can be a grueling exercise. Successfully completing the exam (and then the subsequent oral interviews) requires extensive and intensive knowledge of U.S. and world

Visit Vault at **www.vault.com** for insider company profiles, expert advice, career message boards, expert resume reviews, the Vault Job Board and more.

VAULT CAREER LIBRARY

29

history, international relations and major political issues. Says one foreign service officer who joined in the mid 1990s: "The applicants who do best on the test are those who have literally spent a lifetime preparing for it: They're naturally interested in foreign affairs and world events, have often done their degree in that area, and have followed the news their whole life. This type of background will be invaluable."

Check out www.state.gov for more information on the exam, study hints and guides.

Potential FSOs come from a wide variety of backgrounds, and knowledge of a foreign language is not required (though it will make you a more attractive candidate). In addition to deep knowledge of world affairs, the State Department looks for personal characteristics and traits that will best represent America overseas.

Beyond the Foreign Service, there are other ways to work for the U.S. government abroad. While virtually all the diplomatic staff in a given embassy are transferred Foreign Service professionals from America, a lesser-known option is also available. In addition to local support staff, many of the larger embassies and trade missions will hire locally based Americans, either for the commercial section or for the visa section. Working in the commercial section, you might find yourself facilitating the visit of a key trade group. In the visa section, you would interview potential immigrants to America.

These jobs are not hired for out of country. You will need a valid work permit before you can be considered. Working in this capacity will give you the chance to see the inner workings of the diplomatic world, and test whether a diplomatic career is right for you.

Uppers and downers

The Foreign Service is an excellent training ground and a superior way to see the world. With the world a constantly changing place and an increasingly wide array of international issues – think medical, environmental, social and religious, as well as economic and political – on the agenda, the Foreign Service can provide an exciting and stimulating career path.

The lifestyle and constant rotations have a downside, too, and that is the impact on your personal life. While picking up and exploring a new city and a new job every few years can be exciting in your twenties, the lack of stability can be more problematic as you get older. Having a spouse or partner who is willing to rotate with you is a plus. The State Department is gradually lengthening the time of each rotation, expanding the average to three or four years.

And when all is said and done, the Foreign Service is still part of the government, and works to a government time line. Says one Foreign Service officer: "Your job content may change every few years, but don't expect your seniority or even level of responsibility to grow as quickly as it would in the private sector." The Foreign Service can be bureaucratic and hierarchical. Turnover is low, and as most FSOs are careerists, you have to be prepared to wait and bide your time as you move slowly up in the ranks.

Laura in the Foreign Service

Laura joined the Foreign Service after studying economics for her undergrad degree. She hadn't planned on entering the Foreign Service before college, and in fact didn't even know that it existed. "I've been interested in politics and foreign affairs my entire life. When I was growing up, I traveled and participated in as many exchange programs and study abroad opportunities as I could. When I found out about the Foreign Service, it seemed like a natural fit."

Passing the test was surprisingly easy for Laura, and she credits her success to her lifelong interest in politics. Her advice for acing the exam? "Read like a fiend! Read everything you can – the *Economist*, *The Wall Street Journal*, local papers – and be consistent: don't try to cram a lifetime's of knowledge into a couple of months."

Laura spent seven years in the Foreign Service, mostly in Asia. Joining prior to the days when you had to declare a "track," she spent time in many different areas, including visa work, political analysis and project management. She was pleasantly surprised by the impact of her job and the weightiness of it. "You really feel like you're making a difference. The work that you are doing matters. It's something I haven't experienced again since moving to the private sector." The best thing about the Foreign Service? "The constant change, the chance to reinvent yourself, your career and your location every couple of years. An absolute must for a change junkie like me."

In the end, though, the downside of that same positive led Laura to leave the service. "If you want a career in the Foreign Service, you have to be prepared to deal with the very thing that makes it so exciting in the beginning: the constant change. Frankly, I had a desire for a more "normal" life."

Visit Vault at **www.vault.com** for insider company profiles, expert advice, career message boards, expert resume reviews, the Vault Job Board and more.

V/\ULT CAREER LIBRARY   31

Laura decided to do an MBA immediately after leaving the Foreign Service, but found the transition to the private sector harder than she expected. When recruiting, she found that the skills she had developed or the experiences she had had were in many ways non-transferable. "In the Foreign Service, for example, "analysis" means political analysis. In the business world, analysis refers to crunching the numbers, something of which I had had zero experience – I'd hardly even used Excel! And while recruiters might think it was cool I had experience negotiating with North Korea, how relevant is that to their business?"

Based on her experience, Laura cautions anyone who is considering taking the exam and joining: "Really do your homework and research the life and the work as much as possible. Talk to current officers, both junior and senior. While you don't know who or what you'll be in five years, try as much as possible to make sure it's the career (and the life) for you. Don't jump into it lightly to "see where it leads." It's not that kind of job – this is a job for life."

Development Workers

Who they are

From large development organizations and banks such as the IMF and the World Bank funding giant multi-decade projects, to small NGOs (non-governmental organizations) organizing grass-roots projects, to volunteer agencies providing everything from fence builders to business consultants, global development has become a huge industry.

There is a wide range of opportunities under the "development" umbrella, and just as wide a variety of people working in this industry. Development gurus range from top-level senior executives to junior volunteers straight out of college. Opportunities run from micro-finance to building bridges, from environmental work to helping democracy take hold in remote corners of the world. Many development organizations focus on economic development and financial skills. While there are certainly still opportunities to help villagers build houses, more and more opportunities focus on small business development, nurturing local entrepreneurship and providing sustainable business skills.

Development Lingo

ADB: Asian Development Bank

Fourth World: a group of the poorest countries in the world, that fall below "Third World" and whose economies are stagnating

Green Revolution: agricultural improvements first pioneered in the 1960s

IFC: International Finance Corporation

IMF: International Monetary Fund

Micro-finance, micro-credit: very small loans (sometimes as little as $50) to local entrepreneurs (often women or minorities) to enable them to start small businesses

NGO: non-government organization; a non-profit that acts like a private company

Privatization: the process of a government selling state companies to private companies, who will then (in theory) run them in a leaner, more efficient way than in the past.

Visit Vault at **www.vault.com** for insider company profiles, expert advice, career message boards, expert resume reviews, the Vault Job Board and more.

V/\ULT CAREER LIBRARY   33

> **Sustainable:** development that can be sustained after the aid workers and the loans have been made; the goal of most development projects
>
> **Third World:** developing countries that are growing their economies
>
> **UN:** United Nations

Types of "development" organizations

Development is such a broad term, but the following groups of organizations are generally included under this umbrella:

Public multinationals: Huge organizations like the UN, the World Bank, and the ADB (Asian Development Bank).

Multinational NGOs: Large non-government organizations, such as Amnesty International, CARE, Doctors without Borders and the World Wildlife Fund (WWF)

Smaller NGOs: Hundreds of locally based, often grassroots organizations devoted often to one particular issue or problem, be it women's health, micro-finance or political education.

Volunteer organizations: Organizations that rely on volunteers, though they may pay a stipend.

There are also private companies involved in development work and branches of private companies that work as a non-profit on development-related issues. For example, many of the major consulting and tax consulting companies have arms dedicated to the issues of development, privatization and economic development. Their clients are mainly governments and the public multinationals.

Volunteering is often the first step for many people to get involved in development work, though volunteering can be an attractive option even if you don't envision a long-term career in development. Volunteering, either on a long-term (up to two years) or short-term (a few months) basis is a great way to experience another culture while making a difference.

There are thousands of volunteer opportunities out there, offering you the chance to get involved in whatever your particular passion or geographic preference is. The most famous organization for Americans is the Peace

Corps, but there are numerous other organizations and agencies that offer opportunities for committed volunteers.

Most volunteer assignments are just that: volunteer, meaning you won't be drawing a salary. In some cases, though, you may draw a stipend. A stipend is a living allowance to cover basic necessities, so that while you might not be saving any money, you won't be out of pocket either. Some programs will cover airfare and housing. When evaluating whether or not volunteering is feasible for you, consider loan-forgiveness – many universities have loan-forgiveness programs for graduates who choose to work in the nonprofit sector.

Many volunteer opportunities require you to pay the organization for the opportunity to volunteer. Think seriously about these types of opportunities, especially for "volunteer" programs that are for teaching English. While it is great to have the support these programs offer, you could easily be paid for doing the same work.

Major Volunteer Organizations

Peace Corps: Places over 7,000 volunteers a year. Commitments are for two years, though it is possible to extend them. Check out their comprehensive web site for more details: www.peacecorps.gov

MBA Enterprise: The Peace Corps for the MBA crowd. Places recent MBA grads in positions to act as management and business consultants. Currently heavily focused in central Asia and Eastern Europe. Check out the site for more information on postings, qualifications, and how to apply: www.mbaec-cdc.org

Cross Cultural Solutions: The "mini peace corps," operating in 10 different countries. Volunteer opportunities are short term only (usually 3 weeks) and can be a good way to get your feet wet and see if development work is really for you. Visit the well-organized web site: www.crossculturalsolutions.org

American Friends Service Committee: The Quakers. Has a handful of domestic as well as global (mostly Latin America) opportunities. www.afsc.org

Earth Watch: Organizes "expeditions" where participants get involved in local development and environment issues. Not exactly volunteering,

Visit Vault at **www.vault.com** for insider company profiles, expert advice, career message boards, expert resume reviews, the Vault Job Board and more.

VAULT CAREER LIBRARY

35

but a fascinating way to see development and conservation in action up close. Warning – expensive! www.earthwatch.org

Volunteer Travel: Small outfit offering "vacation" type volunteer programs in 11 countries. www.volunteertravel.com.

Global Services Corps: Operates in Thailand and Tanzania. Volunteers generally stay with a local family. Short-term volunteer programs run year round in health, environment and education. www.globalservicecorps.org.

Global Volunteers: Offers short-term (up to three weeks) placements in 19 different countries. www.globalvolunteers.com.

Use these web sites and directories devoted to volunteering and finding work in the non-profit sector:

www.ciee.org – CIEE (Center for International Education Exchange): Offers numerous volunteer opportunities (over 800 at last check) along with study and travel programs. Their web site is one of the most comprehensive, and has a "program finder" to help you narrow down the choices. Application information and fee information are also included. Use their web site, even if you aren't planning on volunteering with them (some of their programs can be pricey), to get a sense of the range of opportunities and organizations out there

www.idealist.org – One of the premier resources for people interested in development, Idealist is an excellent job board and resource center. Focuses on both domestic and international development.

www.oneworld.net – Another great resource, with jobs, information, country-specific sites, news updates and more. Focus on news and happenings globally. Essential reading (sign up for their newsletter) for anyone interested in development and emerging economies.

www.volunteerabroad.com – One of the largest directories on the web devoted to volunteer opportunities. Doesn't charge organizations to list, so manages to gather smaller organizations and co-ops that wouldn't be able to afford a paid directory. If you can't find it here, it probably doesn't exist. Also traveler information and travel resources.

www.cwis.rg – Center for World Indigenous Studies. Focuses on the "Fourth World" (i.e. more desperate than the Third World). A good source of papers and facts.

> **Also consider the excellent book:** Alternatives to the Peace Corps, edited by Joan Powell, for more ideas.

Qualifications

Development careers can be extremely competitive, especially for entry-level graduates. Many professionals in the field, especially senior-level ones, are hired laterally from private enterprises and bring strong technical and financial skills to their positions.

The more prestigious organizations, such as the IFC (International Finance Corporation), the ADB (Asian Development Bank) or the World Bank, are almost impossible to break into except in very low level, clerical positions. For example, the IFC regularly receives more than 10,000 applicants every year for its two-year Young Professionals program (about 20 are eventually accepted). Being hired by the World Bank out of college requires a degree from a top university as well as excellent connections.

A notch down from the large international development and aid banks are a large number of NGOs and smaller government affiliates. The emphasis for these organizations, which generally keep very lean administrative costs, is to get as much bang for the buck as possible. They are looking for superior technical skills and individuals who can bring as much as possible to the organization. A commitment to, and passion for, human development is also crucial.

If you are looking to enter development, the easiest entrée is via volunteering. While some programs may be competitive, the selection process for voluntary assignments, not surprisingly, is nowhere near as competitive as for paid positions. The Peace Corps has one of the most rigorous selection processes. It can take up to 12 months after the initial application to be accepted into the program.

What do volunteer agencies look for when they place volunteers? Above all, commitment and stamina. For many volunteer positions, job experience and academic accomplishments are less important than a dedication and a passion for what you are about to do. Remember that even though you may be footing the bill for some of your travel and living expenses with various programs, you still represent an investment for a nonprofit organization. They will want to make sure you don't leave before the end of the agreed upon term.

Visit Vault at **www.vault.com** for insider company profiles, expert advice, career message boards, expert resume reviews, the Vault Job Board and more.

VAULT CAREER LIBRARY   37

A Peace Corps recruiter had this to say about their decision criteria: "A successful applicant must be above all committed to the process, and demonstrate their commitment to development. Personal characteristics we look for are flexibility and an adventurous spirit, and an ability to function in a harsher than normal work environment."

Uppers and downers

One of the attractions of development work, of course, is the opportunity to feel like you're really making a difference to the world, in a way that crunching numbers in a cubicle could never match. As Amanda, who worked with an NGO on democracy building in Croatia and Macedonia for three years, says: "Training others to jumpstart the democracy process, and their excitement at the changes happening, was an amazing, formative and mind-opening experience."

In addition to a changed world view and a heightened appreciation for the way the world works and fits together, volunteering in tough conditions overseas can give you skills and develop personality traits that will be useful later in many professional situations. Says one ex-Peace Corps volunteer: "It was a real character building experience. I feel like I draw daily on the skills I learned. Nothing phases me now – I feel like I can accomplish anything, and I'm not thrown by unpredictable variables."

Volunteering can be a smart start to a career as well. There are often opportunities once a rotation is finished, to transition into professional (read, "paying") situations. Because they are often placed in remote areas, Peace Corps volunteers and others working for NGOs are in a great position to learn valuable language skills and gain an in-depth understanding of the culture and the region. The Peace Corps is also changing, and while you still might be digging ditches, an increasing number of projects that require, and develop, business skills are available.

Organizations such as the Peace Corps maintain strong alumni networks that can be helpful in later career development. Says one PC ex-volunteer: "Of the other volunteers I knew in the region, approximately 1/3 have stayed in the development field, another 1/3 have gone on to business school, and another 1/3 have returned to their pre-PC career. In all cases, the alumni were incredibly helpful and supportive."

The downside of volunteering, of course, is the pay (or lack thereof). While most long-term volunteers are provided with a stipend and airfare, if you need to save money or pay off student loans, volunteering is not your best option.

Another downside is more intangible. While it certainly may be possible to see economic change and development in action, the harsh reality, especially for short-term volunteers, is that you won't. Many volunteers suffer from a sense that they have not done much, and find it hard to quantify what their actual contribution was to the community. It's a sad fact, but true: Growth in the development industry has in many cases outpaced the economic development it was supposed to encourage.

Todd in the Peace Corps

Todd joined the Peace Corps after graduating. He explains his motivation: "After growing up in a small town and attending college in the same area, I was looking for adventure. I felt that there would always be time for 'conventional work'." He applied to the Peace Corps as one of his options after graduation, and waited nearly a year for the final approval. The application process was thorough and tiresome, especially the medical part. "At the time, it was a pain. But in retrospect, I think making a long application process makes sense: If you can't survive that, how will you survive in the field? It really tests your dedication."

Todd was placed in a remote village in Paraguay, and spent two years there. He learned Spanish and Guarani (the local Indian language) and, all in all, found the experience to be wonderfully challenging. "It was very, very grassroots. By that I mean there was no roadmap, literally an empty field! If we wanted to do things, we had to do it from scratch, from the ground up. Overall, I was very happy with my experience. I was in a great situation and for the first year at least I was really able to feel like I was having an impact and making a difference."

"I also think I was very satisfied because I had practically no work experience beforehand. The assignment process is rather random, and often we don't know beforehand what skills would be required in a given community. Sometimes, the Peace Corps has a hard time matching skills with situations. So if you don't have any skills, you're fine. But I do know some people who were underutilized and frustrated because they were mismatched, or because the situation they were in did not fit their skill set."

Looking back on his experience, Todd cites the following benefits: "I think the international perspective I gained was really valuable. The language skills are great. We did a lot of fundraising and capital raising

Visit Vault at **www.vault.com** for insider company profiles, expert advice, career message boards, expert resume reviews, the Vault Job Board and more.

VAULT CAREER LIBRARY   39

for irrigation projects, and I was able to develop skills in some of the managerial areas like fundraising and project management."

One of the best aspects, adds Todd, is the alumni network: "In every city you go to, there is a strong network of alumni. And it's probably unlike any other 'alumni network' – we didn't just go to the same school and cheer the same sports teams for four years. We have a very strong bond, because we were all in incredibly difficult, challenging situations, and we were all there because we wanted to make a difference. It's incredible to have that group of people so concentrated in one place."

Entrepreneurship

Who they are

If you're not adventurous to the core, don't read any further. But if you're part of that that rare group of adventurous souls with entrepreneurial impulses starting a company in a foreign country is a doubly courageous effort with extreme risks – and rewards.

Entrepreneurial opportunities abound overseas. Many developing countries have economies growing at faster rates than in the West. And as economies grow, their populations start to crave consumer services and products that didn't previously exist. These changes create opportunities for wily entrepreneurs.

Today, many of the leading consumer companies are making most of their profits overseas in emerging economies like India and China, where the appetite for such consumer products as shampoos, toothpastes, soups and cleaning products is growing exponentially. As markets mature, foreigners are often in a great position to introduce trends, products and services from their home markets that might be suitable overseas.

There are two main types of entrepreneurs discussed in this section:

1.   The importer/exporter

2.   The "homegrown" entrepreneur

The importer/exporter

While not strictly "working" overseas (at least not full-time), an importer brings into the country goods from other countries to sell domestically. Importation is a huge business: Much of what we wear, eat and use was made overseas and imported into the United States. A brief overview of the mechanics of importation follows.

First, you need to find a supplier in the country of origin that will supply you with the product you want to import. You may choose to bring the merchandise back yourself on the plane. If the product is bulky or you have purchased too much to fit in a reasonable amount of personal luggage, you then need to ship the goods back. You will rent space in a container on a ship to transport your product to the United States. If you are in the country, you can supervise the loading and the packing of your container yourself. Or you can contract the services of a freight forwarder, who will supervise the movement of your goods from the point of purchase all the way into the United States (or wherever you're shipping to).

Back in the United States, you need to find a place where your product will reach your potential customers. If you are importing a consumer good (as opposed to a product aimed at other businesses) you will need to set up a retail outlet. This could either be your own store, or a virtual storefront on the Internet (your own web site or an auction site like eBay), or you could distribute your product to a variety of other retailers who have agreed to carry your product.

For example, if you are importing pottery from the south of France, you probably won't want to start your own retail store that exclusively carries this one product. This would involve expense and time that you might not have, not to mention the fact that a store that only carried pottery might not be very attractive to potential customers. Instead, you would want to find a number of established retail arts and crafts stores that will carry your product. Finding these stores can be your own job (walking into likely stores and presenting your business and your product), or you could work through a sales representative.

Sales reps do exactly what their name implies: They represent various products. They carry products from suppliers (in this case you) and distribute them out to a wide variety of retail outlets where they have contacts. The sales reps help you place your products in the right stores and into a greater number of stores and outlets than you would be able to on your own. But their services don't come cheap, and you need to make sure you have a large

Visit Vault at **www.vault.com** for insider company profiles, expert advice, career message boards, expert resume reviews, the Vault Job Board and more.

VAULT CAREER LIBRARY   **41**

enough quantity of goods, selling at a large enough mark-up, to warrant their services.

When considering an import business, the first thing you need to familiarize yourself with are the legal and custom regulations around your proposed product of import. Some products are heavily taxed when coming into the U.S., and this will make a significant difference to your profit calculations.

If you are completely new to the import business, and considering a business where you will actually be bringing goods into the country (as opposed to selling directly via a "virtual" storefront on the web) you might want to consider working with an import/export company for six months to a year. This will enable you to learn the ropes before you start your own venture.

What part of the import business is the easiest to get into? It depends, of course, on your background and your skill set (we wouldn't recommend getting involved in ball bearings, for example, unless you've worked for a couple of engineering firms and know exactly how they are bought and sold!) but some products are easier to import than others. Some artisanal products like arts and crafts, some clothes and novelty items can be small-scale businesses that are easy to break into. The first steps? Identify the product you want to import, meet some potential suppliers (either in country or at trade shows) and find out the custom regulations.

The reverse of the importer, the exporter takes goods from the States and brings them to a foreign country to sell directly.

This can be more complicated than importing into the United States. You will be dealing with most of the bureaucracy and retail issues (distribution, quotas, bureaucracy, tariffs and taxes) in a foreign country that you are not familiar with. In this case, it is almost essential to have a local partner, or at least a deep and thorough knowledge of the local market and business culture.

In most cases, the exporter brings a product from the West that is not commonly available in other countries. Because most countries outside the United States and Europe have lower standards of living, exporting on a small scale works best for goods that are either targeted at the high end of the market, or are very unique (and also usually expensive).

Importing Wine to China

John and Jake were two American management consultants who had worked in China for a few years. After working on a project for the emerging Chinese wine industry, the two decided to start their own company importing California wines to China. They planned to open their own retail store, as well as distribute their imports to restaurants and upscale supermarkets.

They calculated they would be successful because China did not have a quality domestic wine industry, and because the rapidly emerging middle class was consistently drawn to new and novel "American" status symbols – including wine.

Although the market when they started was small, they calculated that it would grow rapidly. Their biggest obstacle? Dealing with the constantly changing Chinese bureaucracy. Says Jake: "The number of rules and regulations surrounding import of beverages, alcoholic beverages, fruit and foodstuffs was unbelievable, and appeared to change daily. Getting a grip on what we could and couldn't do was a real challenge." The two persevered. Now, one of the fundamental predictions that they based their business plan on has come true: Wine consumption among domestic Chinese has skyrocketed.

The Import/Export Box of Terms

Tariff: "Duty" (i.e., a fee) imposed by the destination country on products being imported.

Quota: A fixed amount of a given product that can be imported (or in some cases, exported) within a certain time frame.

Customs: The government department that controls what comes in and goes out of the country.

Quarantine: A period of isolation that animals, and sometimes plants, need to undergo before being allowed to enter the country.

Freight Forwarder: More than a shipping agent, a freight forwarder essentially takes care of getting your product from A to B. They might pick up merchandise at a factory, load it into a container on a ship, and even deliver it forward beyond the port of entry into the country. An indispensable part of the import/export supply chain.

Visit Vault at **www.vault.com** for insider company profiles, expert advice, career message boards, expert resume reviews, the Vault Job Board and more.

VAULT CAREER LIBRARY   43

Resources for Importer/Exporters

On the Web are a number of trade exchanges that bring together buyers and sellers of a wide variety of products. Some of these are more focused on industrial, B2B products, but they are also a good source of information about the way the business works:

- www.alibaba.com: The largest portal for goods.

- www.export-all.com: Despite the name, deals with both importing and exporting.

- www.internationaltrade.com: Focuses on industrial goods.

- www.uschamber.com/International: Resource with lots of information regarding international trade.

- www.buyusa.gov: Government sponsored web site. Lots of detailed information on specific countries.

In addition to Web resources, check out these books:

- *Building an Import/Export Business,* by Dr. Kenneth B. Weiss
- *How to Start an Import/Export Business: Your Step by Step Guide to Success* by Rob Adams and Terry Adams.
- Lots of practical advice from *Entrepreneur Magazine's* "Start Up" series of books.

Homegrown entrepreneuers

The second type of entrepreneur profiled is what we'll call the "homegrown" entrepreneur. This refers to the intrepid individual who sets up a company overseas that is local to the country in question (i.e., doesn't involve an import/export component). Of course, whenever westerners go overseas and set up a business, they are in a sense "exporting" their ideas and their knowledge.

Why start a business overseas? In addition to the macroeconomic factors already talked about, Americans often have some intangibles that can make them successful entrepreneurs. In many countries, the entrepreneurial ideal of starting a business by oneself may be frowned upon or looked down upon from a social standpoint (small business owners may have no standing in the community or within their families), and also from an economic standpoint (banks won't consider loaning to small businesses).

What type of company can you start? It could be anything, but usually falls within one of two categories:

1) Starting a business centered around a specific expertise/talent you have that is lacking overseas.

2) Introducing a service that is successful in the West but hasn't hit it big where you are. For example, gyms and bodybuilding are just beginning to become mainstream in many parts of Asia.

The Western entrepreneur capitalizes on these differences by introducing into a foreign market a concept or service that has proven to be successful at home.

Where are the best countries to start a business? It depends on what you're planning to do. If you're researching an ideal location to start a business, look at the demographic and economic trends. In addition, make sure you have a very good feel for the country and culture.

Resources for Entrepreneurs

There are many resources on the web for entrepreneurs, with help on writing business plans, securing loans and growing your business. Most of them are not aimed toward international businesses. Nonetheless, the resources and information available can be useful in all contexts.

- www.entrepreneur.com
- www.EntreWorld.com
- www.ideacafe.com
- www.inc.com

There are numerous books available that cover all aspects of starting your own business. Again, there aren't any that specifically look at starting a business in a foreign country, but the information inside will be helpful in many respects. Check out the *Vault Guide to Starting Your Own Business*.

Visit Vault at **www.vault.com** for insider company profiles, expert advice, career message boards, expert resume reviews, the Vault Job Board and more.

VAULT CAREER LIBRARY   45

Qualifications for entrepreneurs

There are no formal qualifications to make you a successful entrepreneur, though all and any knowledge of business and finance is always a plus. But the most important characteristics are intangible: drive, ambition, flexibility, creativity and independence. And don't forget gumption, guts and an adventurous spirit. As discussed above, many Americans have these qualities, making them valuable engines for global innovation.

In addition to the requisite personal attributes, it also helps to have the following when thinking of starting a new business in a foreign country:

• **Local partner**: It's always essential to have at the very least local connections, and hopefully a local partner. This will help you understand the logistics and the mechanics of the business in another part of the world, and it will also gain valuable connections and insider knowledge that are often extremely important in doing business in other parts of the world. Unlike the more regulated and clinical business relationships of the United States, for example, many other cultures rely to a large degree on personal connections and building the right relationships with the right people. Having a local partner is the first step toward getting the right "in" in the market.

• **Knowledge of the local market:** This is business and entrepreneurial essential. It's helpful if you've lived in the country for a while before thinking about launching a business there. Most entrepreneurs who start a business in a foreign country do have significant experience in that country before striking out on their own. For example, Josh and Jake, profiled above, worked as consultants in Shanghai before starting their own wine importing business to cater to the emerging Chinese middle class. Another American entrepreneur, John, taught English in Thailand and studied at a local business school before pioneering a "Zagat's" style guide to Bangkok. Now he is on his way to building a successful media company.

• **Deep pockets:** No matter what your initial financial forecasts are, you'll probably need more money than you anticipated. Also keep in mind that, unless you have a local partner, reputable funding may be harder to come across outside your native land where you don't have well established credit history. In some countries the concept of personal credit is not developed and banks are not in the business of lending to entrepreneurs. As for an American bank lending to a business (albeit American-owned) that plans to operate in another country? In a word (or two) – forget it!

The Cost of Setting Up a Business Abroad

So is starting a business abroad less costly than at home? The answer, of course, depends. It depends on what type of business you're considering, and where you want to start it. The following broad guidelines will give you a rough idea of some of the comparative costs involved.

While prices in most parts of Europe and Japan are just as or more expensive than in North America, most of the rest of the world is less expensive to do business in. In many developing countries, these items from your income statement and balance sheets will represent significant savings for you over a similar situation in America:

- **Labor, especially unskilled.** One of the major reasons why so many multinational companies have factories in less developed nations like Indonesia, China and India. Wages in some countries are still just cents a day.

- **Rent.** With some exceptions, in general local-style office space and production facilities will be cheaper on a comparable basis.

- **Basic materials.** Important if you're thinking of manufacturing or importing basics.

- **Transport.** If you're on a well established route, transport costs can be less expensive.

- **Daily living and personal expenses.** A consideration during the early days when you're in the "struggling entrepreneur" phase!

But even though the overall cost of living in a country may be a lot lower than in the States, and even though you might be saving in some areas, watch out for these possible hidden costs:

- **Transport:** If you're on a less well-established route, this can add significantly to your costs. You'll also be paying more in insurance and aggravation: Breakdowns, thefts and weather making roads or waterways impassable are all more common in developing countries.

- **Qualified labor:** While hiring unskilled labor is definitely cheaper, if you want to hire a senior, qualified foreigner, you might have to put up the full "expat package." Do you want to hire a qualified local? Yes, you and every other foreign-

Visit Vault at **www.vault.com** for insider company profiles, expert advice, career message boards, expert resume reviews, the Vault Job Board and more.

VAULT CAREER LIBRARY

47

owned company in the country. In some countries, there is an extreme imbalance between the demand for professional local skills and the supply, driving up labor costs for qualified locals.

- **Bureaucratic costs in time and headaches:** While time might not show up as a line on your Income Statement, you need to factor in the fact that probably nothing will happen as fast as you originally forecast.

- **Need for a local partner:** For certain industries in some countries, having a local partner is more than just good business sense: It's a legal necessity. In this case, you might have to do a joint venture with a "sleeping" local partner that doesn't do anything but lend his name to your registration. The legal costs associated with setting this up then need to be considered.

- **Corruption and bribery:** In many countries, a standard of doing business, and one you should try to estimate beforehand. Talk to other foreign businesses. In what cases have they had to "smooth things over?" And how much did it cost?

- **Taxes:** Higher in some countries than in the United States.

- **Rent:** If you need a prominent, central address for your office location, rents for prime office space in major urban cities, even in ones with relatively cheap overall living standards like Mexico City or Shanghai, can be even more than in downtown Manhattan.

Uppers and downers for entrepreneurs

The benefits of starting your own business abroad are akin to the benefits of being an entrepreneur at home, only intensified. The entrepreneurial high comes from the satisfaction of creating something, of being your own boss and of being in control of decision making. With an international business, there are other potential benefits, such as having an impact on the local economy and creating jobs. The sense of accomplishment can also be enhanced, simply because the barriers to success are often greater abroad. And, of course, like with all entrepreneurial ventures, there can be serious money to be made.

The downside of being an entrepreneur abroad include an increased risk of failure due to the complications of attempting to do business in another culture. Corruption is often a significant factor, as well as an over-zealous bureaucracy, a shortage of skilled labor, infrastructure and telecommunications headaches, and plain cultural differences in doing business.

A word of caution: If you haven't started your own business at home, you may want to try something domestically first. Being an entrepreneur is not glamorous, and it is a lot more work than even the most pessimistic planner might realize. You don't want to get an ugly surprise about the real side of entrepreneurship at the same time as you are dealing with culture shock and navigating an unfamiliar business environment.

Michael in Bolivia

Michael runs a telecommunications company in Bolivia. While living and working in Miami, he met a friend who was originally from Bolivia. The friend had worked for a while in the United States but had decided he was interested in going back to Bolivia. "We had talked about starting a business together, and then we thought about starting something in Bolivia together. Why not? Miguel knew the lay of the land, start up costs were cheaper and there seemed to be a lot of things we could make a start at that hadn't already been done there."

"I went down with him on vacation, and everything just sort of gelled. Based on their combined experience in telecommunications and technology, they decided to start a software company. "At first it was tough, but we knew it was going to be. I think our expectations were pretty in line with what happened. And having Miguel as a partner was simply indispensable – I couldn't have done it alone. It was the perfect combination – I had the technical expertise, and he knew the local market."

Michael found that knowing the local language was also invaluable. "I knew Spanish from having grown up and lived in Miami for many years, and while I certainly wasn't fluent before I got there, I certainly improved fast. And I can't imagine doing what we did without speaking Spanish – of course my partner spoke, but I'm so glad I did too. It gives you a much greater comfort level than if you have to rely on hearing everything second hand. You feel more in control, and more in the know."

Visit Vault at **www.vault.com** for insider company profiles, expert advice, career message boards, expert resume reviews, the Vault Job Board and more.

VAULT CAREER LIBRARY   **49**

Their biggest challenge? Dealing with an uneducated labor pool and with corruption. "Bolivia has corruption problems, and while we knew it was going to be a challenge I would say we were somewhat unprepared for the depth of the problem! Also, Bolivia is a very, very poor country and the majority of the work force is uneducated, so getting quality workers is difficult." But all in all, it has been a good experience, and now in their fourth year, Michael and his partner have expanded their software company and started another company, this time in telecommunications.

"In some ways, Bolivia is a less controlling society than America. In the States, the banks wouldn't have looked twice at us – we were too small, and too young, and too risky. Here, things are more unstructured."

Casual Workers

Who they are

Want to pick grapes in France? Work in a pub in London? Join a German family on vacation and look after their children? Thanks to short-term work visas there are a large number of Americans working abroad in short-term, "vacation-type jobs." Most are students or recent graduates, and almost all are in unskilled positions such as pub work, au pairing, agricultural harvest, and short-term clerical jobs. Most of these workers are found in Europe and Australia/New Zealand.

These programs provide individuals with valid work permits for a specific country, but actually finding the job is up to you. Unlike other "intern" programs (described in the next section under "Students") these programs don't require that you have a traineeship or a job set up before you go. With these flexible work permits you enter the country, and then look for a job.

In return for an application fee (ranging from $40 to $250), the two organizations listed below will provide you with a short-term work visa, and offer support both pre and post departure: helping you find a place to stay, putting you in contact with others on the program, providing job leads and support services once you are in the country.

BUNAC – British Universities North America Club. BUNAC offers short-term visas for work in "vacation style" jobs such as bartending or au-pairing. www.bunac.com.

CIEE – Center for International Education Exchange. In addition to study abroad programs, CIEE also offers short-term work visas for Australia, New Zealand, Canada, France, Ireland and Germany. Check out their comprehensive web site – click on the "Work Abroad" button. www.ciee.org

Opportunities for au pair work in Europe can be found on the following web sites:

www.aupairforum.com

www.greataupair.com.

Qualifications

Most participants in temporary work abroad types of programs are either students looking for summer employment between semesters or recent graduates. There is an application process, but unless something is seriously amiss on your application (having been convicted of a crime will make getting a visa almost impossible) you should have no problem being accepted.

You might want to consider going this route if you are looking for a short stay in a European country, either for the summer or a few months after graduation (you are eligible up to six months after you graduate).

You don't need many qualifications, and there is also a great deal of turnover with casual jobs. Getting hired quickly (within a few days or a few weeks) won't be difficult, as long as you aren't too picky.

Uppers and downers

While many workers take casual jobs more to experience the culture rather than gain any significant work experience, working in any type of international job can be a valuable exercise. It's a good way to whet the appetite and open your eyes to the possibilities of living abroad with a no-hassle visa provided and good in-country support systems.

The downside is the short-term duration of the work, and its unskilled nature – although international experience is never a detriment on a resume, working in a pub in London might not do much for your resume or your overall career goals. According to BUNAC, over 80 percent find temporary "summer" employment in service industries, while only a handful find professional or office work. But if a summer of fun and meeting new people, while covering your expenses, is what you're after, then this could be the way for you to go.

Visit Vault at **www.vault.com** for insider company profiles, expert advice, career message boards, expert resume reviews, the Vault Job Board and more.

VAULT CAREER LIBRARY

51

In order for you to continue working in the country, you would have to be sponsored for a new work visa. The short-term work visas described above cannot be extended unless the company you are working for decides to go through the process themselves and sponsor you. As this is generally expensive and time consuming, most casual employers will not go through the hassle. If you want to stay on and work, you might be out of luck.

In fact, according to one co-coordinator at BUNAC, the reason the governments of the countries in question participate in these types of programs is on the strict understanding that they are for temporary stay only and are "not used to get their foot in the door." You could theoretically use your time on your short-term visa to network into a full-time job, of course.

Students

Who they are

While technically not "working," students are a big international presence. The number of American students enrolled in study-abroad programs has almost doubled from 50,000 to almost 90,000 over the past decade. This number does not include American students enrolled directly in foreign universities or studying in non-academic programs.

In order to study outside your home country, you will need a student visa. To get a student visa, you must study at an accredited educational institute that can legally sponsor you for this visa. What "accredited" means differs by country and local law. Make sure, especially if you are planning on studying at a non-academic institute, that the institute in question is in fact legally able to sponsor you for the student visa. This will help you avoid hassles or potential disappointment at the airport.

A student visa is granted to study only the approved course of study at the original educational institute that sponsored you for the visa. It does not legally allow you to work in the country, or study at another institution. Because of their flexible schedule, though, many students do take up illegal, "under the table" work such as teaching private English lessons. For this type of illicit work, sometimes a student visa is preferable to a tourist visa: A student visa is generally issued for a longer period of time than a tourist visa, and renewing a student visa does not usually raise suspicion.

Studying abroad can be expensive. In some cases, tuition at universities abroad will be higher than what you are paying at home. In addition, you need to factor in costs associated with travel, moving, accommodation, and taking care of your stuff back home. Financial aid is available to cover international study, and some American universities have small stipends available to students to cover such work experiences.

There is a dizzying array of programs that can take students abroad for various lengths of time. Included in this category are work abroad programs geared toward current students and recent graduates, as well as traditional academic study programs. The wide array of options can be grouped into a few categories:

- Study abroad, either through your university or via an independent organization

- Direct enrollment in a university abroad

- Internship/work exchange programs

Study abroad programs

An easy and structured way to go abroad, these programs offer the chance to study abroad for a finite period of time. The course of study may be related to your academic major and be for credit.

When looking to study abroad, you can choose to either attend an independent program that is not affiliated with a university or college, or you can explore your own institution's study abroad exchange programs. You need to be a currently enrolled or a recent graduate to be eligible for campus programs.

Independent (Unaffiliated)

Offered by independent (often nonprofit) organizations, these programs are devoted to enhancing cross-cultural understanding. They typically offer a great deal of help and assistance, both pre- and post-departure. Go with one of the larger, reputable organizations. Many independent (unaffiliated) programs are open to recent graduates as well as current students.

If you're planning on going with an independent organization, you need to be certain that the course you will be taking can be taken for credit and fits in well with your major. If you are exploring these programs by yourself, make sure you talk with your academic counselor to get approval that you will be granted credit for the proposed course of study.

Visit Vault at **www.vault.com** for insider company profiles, expert advice, career message boards, expert resume reviews, the Vault Job Board and more.

VAULT CAREER LIBRARY   **53**

Affiliated with your university

If you are a current student, chances are your university has agreements with various international schools where you might have the option of spending a semester or even a year abroad. Unlike the study abroad programs discussed above, these exchanges are arranged directly via your university and not through an outside for-profit or not for profit organization.

If none of the existing programs appeal to you, some colleges and universities will work with you to make your own customized programs that fulfill the necessary academic and course credits.

Direct enrollment

A second option for studying abroad is direct enrollment in a foreign university to pursue your entire degree abroad. Though it is much more common for foreign students to study at an American university than it is for Americans to study outside of the country, it does happen. Most direct enrollment in a foreign university happens in Canada and certain parts of Europe, including England.

Your motivation might be financial, but don't expect significant savings on your tuition bill (except in Canada). Make sure you do your homework – some foreign credentials may not be accepted at home, and this can cause problems later if you plan to apply to grad school.

Direct enrollment can be an attractive option if you are pursuing language or non-academic courses. In this case, you will have probably already graduated from college, and won't be looking for academic credit. Language students often choose to directly enroll in courses, either affiliated with a university or school, or at an independent organization. This enrollment will qualify you for a full-time student visa.

If you are looking to study something non-academic, you may consider a course of study that is related to cultural or artistic programs. For example, you could opt to study yoga in India, or Balinese dance in Bali. You may do this either for the experience and the chance to immerse in another culture, or for the purposes of getting a student visa that allows you to work under the table. While we do not recommend or encourage this, it is certainly very common in many countries.

Internship programs

Internship programs are another option for students currently enrolled in American institutions or recent graduates who want to go abroad. While technically not studying, these programs are all geared toward current students looking for practical short-term work experience, an internship or a traineeship. Most are short-term (three months) but some can be for up to 24 months.

The programs discussed below are usually affiliated with an educational institute and offer practical training and internships. Many of these programs are reciprocal, meaning that as an American if you go abroad, there will be a foreign student coming to America as well. Many are nonprofit. In most cases, actually finding the internship is up to you.

When you join, the organization gives you access to a database, directory and support for finding your internship. Once you have secured your placement, the organization will help you with the necessary work authorization papers.

Many of the following programs offer study, internship, combined study/ internship and volunteer opportunities. Highlighted below are some of the larger ones:

AISEC: The largest student organization in the world. Completely run by students. Arranges for traineeships in more than 85 countries. Check out the web site or the club on campus: www.aiseconline.net

Brethren Colleges Abroad: Organizes over 100 study abroad programs via 20 academic study centers in 17 countries. www.bcanet.org

CDS International: A nonprofit organization geared toward international practical training, fellowship and placement opportunities for young professionals and students. Serves over 50 countries. www.cdsintl.org

Center for Study Abroad: Private non-profit organization offering study abroad programs (not necessarily for academic credit) in 20 countries. Cheaper than other privately offered programs. The programs are not only for college students, but also for working adults, retirees, and other non-students. www.centerforstudyabroad.com.

CIEE (Center for International Education Exchange): The largest organizations devoted to international exchanges, the CIEE offers an extremely wide menu of study abroad, intern, teach and volunteer programs, and has a handy search function to help you narrow down your interest. www.ciee.org

IASTE: IASTE (International Association for the Exchange of Students for Technical Experience) is focused on undergrads in technical fields such as engineering and computing. This program is supported by the UN and offers short-term work exchanges and internships in over 80 countries around the world. www.iaste.org

Global Experiences: Private company offering combination study and internship programs, including marketing and business-oriented courses. Limited number of countries, and a guaranteed work placement. www.globalexperiences.com

U.S. State Department: Internships, mostly unpaid. Very competitive. Check out the web site for information on their internships and fellowships, as well as a host of internationally related material. Great links for travel information, country profiles and services provided to Americans abroad. www.state.gov

The following online directories have information on various programs and the organizations that sponsor them:

www.collegeabroad.com. Database exclusively for college programs, searchable by category.

www.iiepassport.org. Sponsored by the Institute of International Education (administrators of the Fulbright), the site offers a thorough database of study abroad options. Visit their sister site, www.iie.org, for information on the Institute and other programs and fellowships.

www.internabroad.com. Part of the large GoAbroad.com series of web sites that offers some of the largest directories on the web.

www.internationalstudent.com. This "one-stop shop" for students going international with information on travel, insurance, medical issues, housing, and applications also offers application and resume writing services. Good discussion boards and chat rooms on a variety of topics.

www.studyabroad.com. Directories for high school students, college students and post-graduate programs. Good organization of the bewildering number of choices.

www.worldwide.edu. A large international consortium of schools. Has information on 10,000 schools in 109 countries.

Qualifications

Qualifications for the wide variety of options described above will of course vary tremendously by type of program. Some are merit based, while others require little more than the program fee and a GPA of 2.75 or higher. Don't be fooled, though, by minimum requirements: If the program is competitive, the minimum GPA will not be sufficient.

Make sure studying abroad is right for you. Weigh the financial considerations, and think seriously if you should study abroad or wait until you graduate to work internationally.

Talk to your guidance counselor and to the office of international programs at your college. Look for other students who have gone through the same or a similar program and ask about their experiences.

Uppers and downers

Being a student in another country can be a rewarding and challenging experience. As discussed previously, it's definitely the best way to learn a language if that is your interest. Many courses of study, be it business, or political science, or history, or anthropology, also benefit from time spent overseas and a broadening perspective. Being a student abroad can be the ultimate educational experience: You're constantly learning, both in and out of the classroom.

As a student you will probably have a more relaxed lifestyle, with more time to experience the local culture outside of the classroom. Consequently, students often emjoy a fuller cultural experience than professionals working overseas.

Other benefits of being a student are the great networking opportunities that can help you get a job in the country upon completion of your studies, or if you choose to return later. Finally, if a long-term international career is your goal, studying abroad shows you are serious about that goal.

What's the downside of studying abroad? Expense is one, of course. And if you're planning on studying at a local university, expect the unexpected: Dorm rooms and amenities may not be the same as back home. Some campuses overseas are more restrictive than what you're used to. Many universities have rules regarding visitors, dorm activities and schedules, and some even have curfews.

Visit Vault at **www.vault.com** for insider company profiles, expert advice, career message boards, expert resume reviews, the Vault Job Board and more.

V∧ULT CAREER LIBRARY   **57**

Finally, consider what you may be missing back home. You will miss out on your classmates' experiences, and when you return may sense or feel some dislocation. Reverse culture shock may be a difficult thing to deal with if you are concentrating on writing your final thesis.

Rachel, Studying Abroad

Rachel always knew she wanted to study abroad: "To me, there was no other choice. I was born an explorer and have taken every opportunity available to me to travel." In her junior year of undergraduate study, Rachel decided to study abroad. She chose France because she had been studying the language since the 3rd grade: "I figured it was the perfect way to polish up my French and immerse myself in another culture while continuing with my degree."

Unlike most study abroad students, Rachel decided to go abroad for a full year: "I felt the disruption entailed (moving, visas, transcripts, etc.) for just 3 months or so of study was really not worth it. If I was serious about understanding France, and getting the most out of the experience, then I felt I needed a longer time away." With the help of the State university system of New York, Rachel was able to cobble together a double semester, full-year program to continue her studies for the first 6 months in Grenoble, in the south of France, and then in Paris.

She is glad she started outside of Paris: Grenoble, she says, was a better way to be introduced to French culture. "It's a great student city, and I lived with a French family. It took some trying, but I managed to get away from the other students outside of the classroom, make an effort to speak French and make French friends – including a French boyfriend!" If she hadn't tried so hard, admits Rachel, it would have been very easy to study with other Americans and hang out with them in the evenings. And when she moved to Paris, that actually happened. "Paris was completely different from Grenoble. While it was a fascinating city, I'm nonetheless glad I started off in a smaller city; otherwise I don't think I would have had the depth of experience and the close contact with the "real" France that I managed to have in Grenoble."

The upside of studying abroad? A powerful sense of accomplishment and achievement, as well as a renewed appreciation for her own culture and a heightened worldview. Would she do it again? "Absolutely."

Where the Opportunities Are

CHAPTER 3

In the previous chapter we looked at some industries and jobs for Americans overseas. Now let's look at where you might find yourself working. What countries and regions of the world offer the most rewarding experience for the brave, the ambitious or merely the curious? Read on.

International hot spots

Often the decision about where to go is influenced by some combination of the following factors:

- The industry you're looking to work in

- People you know – contacts you already have in a given country

- The language you want to learn and the culture you want to experience

- Your long-term career goals

- Cultural, personal or heritage reasons

Many readers of this book will already have at least a vague idea of where they are interested in going. But if you're still open to ideas and don't have a definite game plan, you may want to consider finding a country or region with long-term opportunities. Some of the following global "hot spots" are fast growing and are (or will be) major economic players on the world stage. All statistics for GDP and population are from 2003.

Argentina

Traditionally one of the economically most stable and politically advanced countries of South America, Argentina underwent a severe crisis in 2001 that left its economy shattered. But it has a good base to rebuild from: extensive infrastructure, rich natural resources and a well-educated population.

Population: 38 million

Language: Spanish

GDP: $10,200

Visit Vault at **www.vault.com** for insider company profiles, expert advice, career message boards, expert resume reviews, the Vault Job Board and more.

VAULT CAREER LIBRARY   59

GDP growth: -14% (due to the economic collapse)

Why it's hot: Rebuilding and restructuring after the collapse of the economy means lots of opportunities for the right people. The economy is still in a bad way, but that will turn around. A country with a fascinating culture and a European heritage, Argentina is a great place to experience South American culture.

What Americans are doing: Banking; working with multinationals; aid, development and international finance organizations

The downside: Volatile economy and political uncertainty. Rising crime due to the recent economic problems and high unemployment.

Living there: Jungles in the north, pampas and glaciers in the south; Buenos Aires; the tango; cheap cost of living and good quality of life

Australia

The "land down under" is under populated with great wide open spaces. The population is concentrated along the coasts and away from the outback (interior). With almost limitless natural resources and extensive farmland, the prosperous, European-style economy is centered around farming and exports.

Population: 20 million

Language: English

GDP: $27,000

GDP growth: 3.6%

Why it's hot: Australia was badly affected by the Asian economic crisis in the late 1990s, but since then has been recovering nicely. The country is hiring for its booming IT and tourism industries. Many multinationals have their Asia Pacific regional headquarters in Sydney.

What Americans are doing: Teaching; working with banks and multinationals; casual work in agriculture and tourism

The downside: The cost of living in places like Sydney can rival New York.

Living there: Beaches, beaches, and more beaches; the outback; fascinating nature and wildlife (all over and inside your house too); outdoorsy culture and relaxed lifestyle.

Brazil

The largest country in South America (and the fifth-largest in the world). A vast multi-ethnic country with extensive natural resources, including the relatively unexplored Amazon Basin. Brazil's economy and domestic market is huge, outpacing that of all the other South American countries combined.

Population: 176 million

Language: Portuguese, some Spanish and English, native dialects

GDP: $7,400

GDP growth: 2%

Why it's hot: With huge natural resources (forests, minerals) and well-developed manufacturing and service sectors, Brazil's economy is a regional and global powerhouse. After an economically troubled decade and extensive financial and economic restructuring, the country is rebuilding.

Americans are working in: Teaching English; media and entertainment; Trade and import/export; manufacturing

The downside: Highly unequal income distribution and rampant poverty. Exploitation of natural resources and ethnic tensions with traditional Indian groups is rising. Brazil is the only country in Latin America that speaks Portuguese (the rest speak Spanish).

Living there: Beach paradise Rio de Janeiro; the Amazon; cheap cost of living; fantastic nature and wildlife; diverse ethnicity and truly multicultural society.

China

A massive economy of more than 1 billion people. After a rocky ride in the 20th century, China's economic reforms over the last 20 years have yielded significant growth. With the Communist Party in power continuously, China is politically communist, but economically becoming increasingly capitalist.

Population: 1.2 billion

Language: Mandarin Chinese (north), Cantonese (South)

GDP: $4,600

GDP growth: 8% (official estimates)

Visit Vault at **www.vault.com** for insider company profiles, expert advice, career message boards, expert resume reviews, the Vault Job Board and more.

VAULT CAREER LIBRARY

61

Why it's hot: China's economy is the second largest in the world after the United States. GDP has quadrupled since 1978 when the government decided to relax internal control and open the country up to outside investors. With a huge domestic market, China has attracted many foreign companies – most Western companies now have some sort of presence there. While many are still struggling to be profitable, there is no doubt that opportunities in China will continue to increase. With the Olympics slated to be held in Beijing in 2008, the demand for English is soaring.

What Americans are doing: Studying Chinese; teaching English; working in consulting and professional services; manufacturing; other service sector industries; education and law

The downside: Corruption is endemic, so starting your own business could be a challenge. Poverty and social unrest seem to be increasing. Much of the centrally controlled socialist policies have resulted in an older workforce that is unproductive, and unemployment and underemployment are rising. Bureaucracy is intrusive and omnipresent.

Living there: The Great Wall, Beijing, cheap internal flights, Tibet, delicious food and fascinating culture and history

The Czech Republic

The Czech Republic, after decades under Soviet rule, was formed when Czechoslovakia split into the Czech Republic and Slovakia. At the crossroads of central Europe, the Czech Republic is rich in history and culture, and has one of the most prosperous economies in the region.

Population: 10.2 million

Language: Czech

GDP: $15,300

GDP growth: 2.6%

Why it's hot: The domestic economy is growing rapidly. There is increasing foreign investment and interest as the government continues to privatize most industries and the country gets ready for entry into the E.U.

What Americans are doing: Teaching English – one of the most popular destinations; working in banking and financial services (most banks are foreign owned); some consumer goods; casual work in bars and tourism; artists and musicians

The downside: Large underground and illegal economy in drugs; high unemployment and some crime. Bureaucracy. Like Poland, the Czech Republic will be joining the E.U. in 2004, resulting in fewer job opportunities for Americans.

Living there: Prague, history, crossroads of Europe, cheap and accessible

France

With a diverse and well-balanced economy, France today is one of the most modern countries in the world and is at the center of the European Union. Like many European countries, France is much more socialist than America and has a 35-hour work week and an extensive social security net (along with high taxes)

Population: 60 million

Language: French

GDP: $25,700

GDP growth: 1.1%

Why it's hot: With a short workweek, and good quality of life, France can be a great place to work. The socialist government has been consistently privatizing many of its key industries, and France boasts companies that are world-class players in many industries, including telecomm, engineering, luxury goods and food.

What Americans are doing: Studying; teaching English; working in tourism and casual jobs; at multinationals and in engineering. Restrictive hiring and firing policies (for all but casual student workers) make getting a job rather difficult without an E.U. passport.

The downside: Vive la France! The French can be very nationalistic and are very proud of their language. Although most professionals and educated people can speak English, you should speak French before looking for a job (other than teaching English).

Living there: Paris, expensive, fantastic food and wine, a chance to experience one of Europe's oldest and most beautiful cultures.

Visit Vault at **www.vault.com** for insider company profiles, expert advice, career message boards, expert resume reviews, the Vault Job Board and more.

VAULT CAREER LIBRARY   63

India

Almost a continent in itself, India is one of the largest and most populous nations in the world. with almost 1 billion people, a huge domestic economy creates a middle class as large as Europe, side by side with severe income disparity and some of the world's worst poverty. The economy runs from traditional village farming, to modern agriculture, to modern industries and professional services.

Population: More than 1 billion

Language: 14 official languages (Hindi is the largest, spoken by 30% of the population) but English is very common and serves as the universal language of commerce amongst the educated class.

GDP: $2,540

GDP growth: 4.3%

Why it's hot: Since 1990, the economy has been growing consistently and many industries are modernizing rapidly. India has some of the world's best scientists and engineers, and a world-class software and IT industry. A well-educated and English-speaking workforce makes it a popular choice for outsourcing and call centers.

What Americans are doing: With so many well-educated and western-educated, English-speaking Indians, traditional opportunities in high tech and consumer goods aren't numerous. Development work with local and international aid organizations/NGOs; teaching English (mostly in call centers); entrepreneurs – as one of the largest economies in the world, India is definitely a place to be for the future; film and entertainment

The downside: Overpopulation, extreme poverty, ethnic tensions and geopolitical instability with Pakistan are some of the problems that characterize this massive and influential nation.

Living there: Major culture shock, limitless places to explore, a chance to get up close and personal in one of the most multiethnic, multilingual and multicultural environments in the world.

Indonesia

A huge, diverse country with hundreds of islands, hundreds of different ethnic groups and a turbulent history, Indonesia characterizes the contradictions of a fast growing, rapidly modernizing country that still seeks to hold on to its traditional roots. One of the largest countries in terms of population, the domestic market is still poor, but holds tremendous potential.

Population: 230 million and growing fast

Language: Bahasa (one of the easiest languages in the world to learn!), English, regional dialects

GDP: $3,000

GDP growth: 3.3%

Why it's hot: A regional powerhouse, Indonesia has undergone recent setbacks and economic difficulties, but prospects for the future should be strong. The government is committed to internal and external reform, and as the Asian region picks up, so will Indonesia.

What Americans are doing: Teaching English; consulting; working in development and pan-Asia initiatives; entrepreneurs; import/export

The downside: Poverty, corruption, some Islamic fundamentalism and recent terrorism, internal strife with the East Timor secessionist movement

Living there: Bali, Bali and more Bali; more islands; very cheap cost of living; colorful, friendly locals, scuba diving and a polyglot, diverse culture

Japan

The most developed and advanced nation in Asia, Japan has an ancient and unique culture. After World War II, Japan grew rapidly and built a robust economy centered around light manufacturing and exports. Recently, Japan has suffered an economic slowdown, but nonetheless remains one of the most important, richest and influential economies in the world.

Population: 127 million

Language: Japanese

GDP: $28,000

GDP growth: -0.3%

Why it's hot: While the economy has been in the doldrums for a decade or so now, Japan still has a huge domestic economy and strong exports. Demand for English remains strong, and opportunities for more foreign involvement and investment are increasing as the economy is forced to become less rigid and more open.

Visit Vault at www.vault.com for insider company profiles, expert advice, career message boards, expert resume reviews, the Vault Job Board and more.

VAULT CAREER LIBRARY

65

What Americans are doing: Teaching English – Japan was and still is one of the world's most popular places to teach; working for multinationals and banks; in entertainment and media; in consulting and professional services.

The downside: With so many Americans speaking and studying Japanese, you will probably need to be fluent before being hired locally for anything but teaching English. A closed and homogenous society, culture shock can be severe. The recent economic stagnation has led to increasing levels of crime (though still very low by American standards). Overpopulation and crowding.

Living there: Experience an ancient and interesting culture up close, Tokyo, the southern beaches, Mount Fuji, drinking and karaoke

Kenya

Traditionally one of Africa's most developed countries, Kenya is a regional hub for trade and finance in East Africa. Since independence from Britain in the 1950s, Kenya has been one of the most politically stable African countries. Ethnically diverse and very beautiful, it nonetheless suffers from many of the traditional blights that affect African countries: reliance on foreign aid to boost the economy, and endemic corruption and bureaucracy.

Population: 31 million

Language: English is the major political and commercial language; Swahili and numerous local dialects

GDP: $1,000

GDP growth: 1%

Why it's hot: Kenya has been having a difficult time since the mid 1990s, and economic growth is slowing. But despite the recent slowdown, Kenya still has better prospects than some of its neighbors and has strong natural resources, tourism potential, and a growing domestic market.

What Americans are doing: Development and economic work; working for NGOs, non-profits, ministry-related or university related organizations.

The downside: Corruption is endemic, and much of the foreign aid money doesn't go where it should. Crime rates are high, and expats and foreigners can be targets for both money and political reasons. AIDS and HIV infection are rampant.

Living there: diverse expat community, cheap food and accommodation, friendly Kenyans, beautiful beaches and fantastic game reserves

Poland

One of the next members of the E.U., Poland is one of the most advanced "Eastern European" countries. Situated between Germany and the ex-Soviet block countries of Eastern Europe, Poland is set to officially become part of Europe when it joins the E.U. (European Union) in 2004. After decades of communist and socialist turmoil, since the 1990s Poland has been pursuing economic policy of economic liberalization.

Population: 39 million

Language: Polish

GDP: $9,500

GDP growth: 1.2%

Why it's hot: Privatization is big on the agenda in Poland, as old state owned firms are bought by private companies (some foreign, mostly from the rest of Europe) and transformed into lean capitalist machines. As a member of NATO, and with admission to the E.U., Poland is becoming a hot place to do business.

What Americans are doing: Teaching English (Poland is one of the top destinations, and while you won't get rich, you'll be able to have a decent lifestyle); working on privatization projects; in banking and consumer goods; entrepreneurs

The downside: Unless you're on an "expat package," wages can be low. Inefficient state structure and lots of bureaucracy. You'll most likely need a knowledge of Polish or Russian to land a job. Once Poland joins the E.U. in 2004, expats from other parts of Europe, including the Germans and the British will probably outnumber Americans as they will be much easier to hire.

Living there: Beautiful beaches, old castles, excellent national parks, hospitable locals

Visit Vault at **www.vault.com** for insider company profiles, expert advice, career message boards, expert resume reviews, the Vault Job Board and more.

VAULT CAREER LIBRARY   67

Russia and CIS

Russia, and the ex-Soviet Union States, now called the Commonwealth of Independent States. The ex-Soviet empire is now 15 independent republics, ranging from the relatively developed ones of Eastern Europe, to some of the wildest areas of the world in central Asia like Kazakhstan and Uzbekistan.

Population: 535 million people (160 million in Russia itself).

Language: Russian is the lingua franca everywhere, with other languages and regional dialects around the region

Per capita GDP: $8,880

GDP growth: Average 5% per year

Why it's hot: After a terrible economic crash in 1996, the economy is recovering and now taking off. Russia is making great strides toward a market economy, restructuring its economic, political and social systems while modernizing its traditional industrial base.

Americans are working in: Teaching English, service sectors, banking, professional services, energy and law

The downside: Corruption is endemic and rampant – a real and serious consideration, especially if you're thinking of starting your own business. Political uncertainty in the central Asian states. Other problems include the lack of a strong legal system, capital flight, and brain drain.

Living there: St. Petersburg and the museums, exploring Siberia, vodka, vodka and more vodka, fascinating history and a people in transition.

South Africa

Emerging after 50 years of apartheid (a strict separation and oppression of the black population by the whites), South Africa today is a fascinating polyglot of a country with a very vibrant culture. The economy is probably the strongest in the region, if not on the continent, but is still hampered by the legacy of apartheid and slowdowns caused by crime and AIDS/HIV.

Population: 43 million

Language: 11 official languages, including English, Afrikaans (the language of the old Dutch settlers), Zulu, and Xhosa

GDP: $9,400

GDP growth: 2.6%

Why it's hot: Southern Africa (and perhaps all of black Africa's) only true developed nation, South Africa has great infrastructure and some of the best roads, ports and telecomm systems on the continent. A great place to enjoy Africa up close and personal while still accessing (at least in major cities!) many of the amenities of the West.

What Americans are doing: Aid and development work; consulting; working with multinationals; volunteering; tourism

The downside: Crime and a high prevalence of HIV/AIDS. Cultural, racial and ethnic tensions.

Living there: Cape Town; the wineries; game parks; jumping off point to explore the rest of southern Africa.

Sweden

The largest (in terms of population) of the Scandinavian countries, Sweden has achieved an enviable standard of living under a mixed system of capitalism coupled with an extensive welfare system. While still reliant on heavy industry and exports of natural resources, Sweden in recent decades has emerged as a world class leader in high tech and telecom. Some of the biggest players in these industries (think Ericsson) are Swedish.

Population: 8.9 million

Language: Swedish, though virtually all educated Swedes speak uncannily perfect English

GDP: $25,400

GDP growth: 1.8%

Why it's hot: Sweden consistently ranks near the top on quality of life ratings. The well-educated, English speaking and cosmopolitan population make living and working here a breeze. The high tech IT sectors, while suffering a bit of a slump these days, is still fundamentally strong and provides one of the strongest engines of growth.

What Americans are doing: IT & software; telecom; banking

The downside: Like many European countries, rigid hiring and firing practices can make it difficult for a non-E.U. passport holder to get a job.

Visit Vault at **www.vault.com** for insider company profiles, expert advice, career message boards, expert resume reviews, the Vault Job Board and more.

VAULT CAREER LIBRARY   **69**

Though most Swedes speak English, knowing some Swedish would give you an good edge. High taxes.

Living there: Socialist paradise up close, Stockholm, smorgasbord and spas

Turkey

A fascinating mixture of East and West, Turkey is strategically located at the border of Europe and Asia – Istanbul, the largest city, is spread across a river that separates the two continents. While heavily Muslim, the state and political system are determinedly secular – a rarity in that part of the world. The economy, though fast growing and rapidly modernizing, is nonetheless still heavily dependent on traditional agriculture.

Population: 68 million

Language: Turkish

GDP: $7,000

GDP growth: 4.2%

Why it's hot: Turkey looks likely to become one of the next invitees to the European Union. This will strongly boost the economy and consolidate its place as an economic leader in the region. The economy, led by strong exports, is fast growing and robust. With the government committed to modernization and structural reforms, the future looks good.

What Americans are doing: Teaching English – more and more Turks are wanting to learn; working for banks and multinationals, working in the export sector.

The downside: Poverty and crime, some political instability and a volatile region

Living there: Beaches on the Black Sea, Istanbul and the bazaars, rich history and an up-close view of Islam in a secular state.

Resources for Country Research

Use the following resources to help you learn more about potential destinations:

- CIA Factbook – www.cia.gov

- Country Profiles – www.about.com

Is an International Career For You?

CHAPTER 4

Does working overseas really lead to exciting jobs and endless opportunities? In many ways, the answer is yes, but as with all things, there is a downside. It's now time for a reality check about going global. Working overseas is not all roses and champagne, or jacarandas and kimchee...

Reasons Not To Go Abroad

Think about your situation carefully before you take the plunge. Working abroad, no matter how cushy the job, and no matter how "Western" a work environment you might think you will find yourself in, will undoubtedly offer more challenges than an ordinary North American work situation. Even if you're transferred overseas and remain with your present employer, it won't be easy. (That's why corporate transfers get hardship pay!)

Moving away from friends and family into a new and strange country can be a traumatic experience. It is almost guaranteed that the first few months, at least, will be very tough. Be prepared for feelings of isolation, loneliness and disorientation.

Because companies can lose millions of dollars if a corporate transfer doesn't work out, a lot of research has been done to identify character traits that lead to success overseas. The theory is that if these traits can be identified, or at least developed, then the risk of an early return home and wasted training will be mitigated. Evaluate your own personality and your chances of success before you go and (potentially) make a costly mistake. Take our test to learn more.

Visit Vault at **www.vault.com** for insider company profiles, expert advice, career message boards, expert resume reviews, the Vault Job Board and more.

VAULT CAREER LIBRARY 73

Personality Traits

The following is a list of the traits that that will help you thrive abroad. While it's certainly not exhaustive, many of these traits are strong indicators of the type of personality that will be successful in another culture:

- Open-mindedness

- Flexibility

- Ability to cope with ambiguity

- Emotional stability

- Intellectual curiosity

- Relationship skills

In addition to possessing the above characteristics, having access to a mentor or a guide is another key success factor.

One leading expert on cross-cultural relocation believes that younger people are more open to change and challenge than older people, and thus naturally possess many of the traits outlined above. For example, they tend to be naturally more adaptive and less fazed by the unexpected than older folks. The flipside is that younger people are sometimes "so focused on being independent that they don't make the sacrifices necessary to be accepted into another culture – the 'no one is going to tell me what I can't do' syndrome."

How adaptive you'll need to be, of course, depends on where you are heading and your job situation. Some countries require more of an adjustment than others to work and live in. If you're not sure about your ability to face a starkly different culture, you might want to consider a stop in Australia, rather than, say, Uzbekistan.

Loneliness

Michelle's experience teaching English in a small town in Korea is typical of the challenges faced by international newbies. "I landed at the airport late at night and was deposited by a representative from the school in a crummy hotel downtown. For three days, before I had to report to work, I stayed like a frightened rabbit inside my hotel room, afraid to venture out, unable to communicate at all with anyone, unable to read any of the signs on the street. If I had had a round-trip ticket (I came on a one way ticket) I would have been very tempted to hop on the next plane back."

Michelle eventually stayed, and made it through her first few months intact. Looking back, she's glad she didn't have that return trip ticket. The experience, she believes, made her a tougher person and more accepting of whatever life might throw at her.

Relationship considerations

Trying to keep a relationship going long-distance can be fraught with difficulties.

Often, a person going alone to a new country will find new distractions, including emotional ones, once they arrive. Add in the personal changes and growth that often happen overseas, and it's not uncommon for many couples to break up in the first few months of a long distance relationship.

Perhaps you are already in a relationship and the two of you are planning to travel together. While this can be a fantastic situation, be aware of the extra strain that such a move can put onto relationships. In situations where only one partner is transferred or has a job offer, the partner who comes along may be unable to find work, have visa problems and/or be overwhelmed by boredom. According to a survey of major American companies who assign employees abroad, the most common factors in assignment failure are partner dissatisfaction (96 percent) and family concerns (93 percent).

If you are planning on going overseas and leaving a partner behind, be realistic. Carefully weigh the pros and cons. If you are going as a couple, think as a pair and try to make as many decisions together as possible. Again, be realistic and manage expectations. If you both know it's not going to be a bed of roses, you'll be better able to identify potential trouble spots.

Visit Vault at **www.vault.com** for insider company profiles, expert advice, career message boards, expert resume reviews, the Vault Job Board and more.

VAULT CAREER LIBRARY

75

Health issues

Sometimes access to even the best medical care another country has to offer will not meet the standards you are accustomed to. If you have a medical condition that does, or may, require a certain standard of care, be sure to prepare for the worst case scenario. Research available medical facilities in the city or town where you plan to work. While cities around the world have medical clinics staffed by Western or Western-trained doctors, they may be limited in the type of care they can provide.

A note on evaluating medical insurance: Make sure you know what situations (e.g. medical evacuation, travel to another city for care, types of doctors covered) are covered by the plan you are considering. Different plans can have varying levels of coverage, so avoid any unpleasant – and costly – surprises.

Risks

Many countries are more volatile than North America, and situations can change rapidly. Before you commit to going anywhere, do the research to make sure you are not putting yourself in unnecessary danger. Understand the history of the region, and check out the U.S. State Department's Consular information sheets. This handy trove of information has current travel advisory warnings as well as information on medical insurance and what to do in case of an emergency.

Once you arrive at your destination, make sure you register with the local embassy. The embassy will facilitate emergency procedures or evacuations if required. But don't expect the embassy to come to your rescue if you have broken the law – in most situations you are subject to all laws of the country in which you are residing. The American Embassy is, in many cases, powerless to intervene if you are convicted of a crime in a local court.

Remember: Even if something is not illegal in the States, it may be illegal in your host country. Follow the local customs and laws. Check out the State Department's web site for complete information on what you can and cannot expect from the local offices at www.state.gov.

Special issues for women and minorities

Gender inequality and overt discrimination can be more of a concern abroad than at home. In many areas of the developing world, women will face a harder time than men. In societies that are more conservative, women are often subject to not-so-subtle expectations about behavior and lifestyle that may translate into a severely curtailed lifestyle.

Even countries that may seem relatively developed and "westernized" still harbor strong expectations about the role of women. Don't expect to be able to smoke on the street in South Korea. Telling a man the name of the hotel you are staying at in Turkey may be considered an invitation to come to your room later.

Women need to take special precautions with clothing. In some societies women are expected to cover their legs and arms, and sometimes their hair. Don't be stubborn, for example, about wearing your favorite sundress if it would be considered too revealing. On the one hand, it's disrespectful to the local culture, and on the other hand, you'll be subject to a lot more harassment than if you dress more conservatively.

When packing, be as conservative as possible. If in doubt, don't bring it. Do yourself a favor and follow the local customs; no matter what your personal beliefs are, you'll have an easier time of it in the end if you try to "blend" rather than resist. One mitigating factor is that American women are often considered "honorary men" and are not subject to the same standards as local women.

Racism can affect all workers abroad. Sometimes, more homogenous and "closed" societies are overtly discriminatory against non-locals. Encountering what amounts to overt discrimination, for many for the first time, can be very challenging. Many foreigners in Japan, for example, have experienced sitting completely alone in a crowded subway car, with two empty seats on either side.

Speaking of the reason why she left one North Asia country after more than four years working as a teacher and in local government, Robin cites the "overt, persistent, systematic, pervasive racism" and the realization that she would never be more than an outsider in the society.

Visible minorities may also face a harder time overseas than Caucasian Americans. While about 25 percent of Americans belong to a visible minority, in the minds of much of the rest of the world all Americans are white. If you're African American, or Chinese American, you might have a hard time getting across the fact that yes, indeed, you really are American and you really can speak English properly!

Even Americans returning to their parents' or grandparents' country can face problems. Many second generation Koreans, for example, find that when

Visit Vault at **www.vault.com** for insider company profiles, expert advice, career message boards, expert resume reviews, the Vault Job Board and more.

VAULT CAREER LIBRARY

77

they return to Korea they are treated as Koreans, and not as Americans, and are expected to speak the language and know and adhere to all local customs.

Common Myths about Working Abroad

Here are a couple of myths about going overseas.

Myth #1: Working internationally is always a good career move.

Despite the opportunities that come with working abroad, they do not always translate into clear-cut advantages. Unless your company transfers you, working overseas can sometimes take you off a more traditional career path, and does not enhance every career goal. For example, if your heart is set on a career in investment banking, taking a few years off to teach English in Prague will not help your professional aims.

Many international experiences, unless they are with a multinational company, are hard to translate into a traditional context. While international experience can help you in getting admitted to graduate school, it is sometimes not useful as preparation for changing careers or finding a job back home.

Myth #2: You can make a lot of money.

Don't go if you're just going for the money. While the potential for making money exists, there are no guarantees. In addition, there are a host of hidden expenses that must be considered in the cost equation.

Check out this list of additional expenses you might face working abroad, especially if your company does not take care of your relocation:

- **Visa**:You might be responsible for obtaining your own work visa, which can cost up to several thousand dollars

- **Health insurance:** If your employer doesn't sponsor you, taking out your own global coverage can be pricey.

- **Travel:** Factor in trips you'll want to make, both back home and in the surrounding region.

- **Phone bills:** Calls home can add up.

- **"Foreigners' tax":** As a Westerner, you will be automatically assumed to be rich, and may be overcharged on everything from taxi rides to rent. This practice is sometimes dubbed the "foreigners' tax."

Myth #3   You'll have a fabulous time.

Before you go, or before you consider going, take an inventory of yourself and your expectations. While this won't prevent you from having a miserable experience, it will help you to manage your expectations.

Answer these questions:

• What are you wanting or hoping to get out of the experience?

• What are your expectations for this experience? Are they realistic?

• What does success and failure mean to you?

• Have you thought through what will happen if things don't work out?

Visit Vault at **www.vault.com** for insider company profiles, expert advice, career message boards, expert resume reviews, the Vault Job Board and more.

V∧ULT CAREER LIBRARY   **79**

Test Your "I.Q" – International Quotient

So... should you stay or should you go? Take this quick quiz to find out. There's no right or wrong answer, but you should be able to answer these questions honestly to yourself.

- Are you single? Y / N

- Will be going with a partner? Y / N

- Have you ever traveled abroad? Y / N

- Have you ever lived abroad? Y / N

- Do you have an interest in other cultures? Y / N

- Are you prepared to not see your family and friends for at least a year? Y / N

- Have you ever experienced real stress or loneliness before in your life? Y / N

- Are you confident of the way you deal with your emotions? Y/ N

- Are you a tolerant person? Y / N

- Do you consider yourself flexible? Y / N

- Do you consider yourself a risk taker? Y / N

- Have you ever felt like an outsider? Y / N

- Do you consider yourself a non-traditional person? Y / N

- Do you have a non-traditional career path in mind? Y / N

- Are you looking at graduate school a few years down the road? Y / N

- Do you have a clean bill of health/are you generally healthy? Y / N

- Do you have enough money to support yourself for at least 3 months without working? Y / N

Count your "yeses" and look on the next page for your score.

Score:

15 + – Go for it!

10-15 – Go for it, but be prepared to be challenged and occasionally
frustrated

5-10 – Think seriously about your plans before you go.

Visit Vault at **www.vault.com** for insider company profiles, expert advice,
career message boards, expert resume reviews, the Vault Job Board and more.

VAULT CAREER LIBRARY   **81**

Use the Internet's
MOST TARGETED
job search tools.

Vault Job Board

Target your search by industry, function, and experience level, and find the job openings that you want.

VaultMatch Resume Database

Vault takes match-making to the next level: post your resume and customize your search by industry, function, experience and more. We'll match job listings with your interests and criteria and e-mail them directly to your inbox.

> the most trusted name in career information™

Practical
Considerations

If you've decided you can thrive and survive away from home, what next? There are a host of practical considerations to consider before planning your strategy for getting an international job.

Work Authorization

As an American, you are entitled to work in America, but outside of your country of citizenship you will need a work permit or work visa in order to be able to work legally. Getting this visa will be one of your single biggest tasks. It could also potentially be one of your biggest stumbling blocks.

All countries in the world require a work visa from foreigners to work in their country. A work visa is different from a tourist visa in that you are legally able to take employment. A tourist visa, by contrast, allows you to be a tourist and nothing more – if you work while on a tourist visa, you're working illegally (see below).

You cannot get a work visa yourself – the company you are working for (or will work for) needs to 'sponsor' you for the visa. This involves time, paperwork and legal fees on the part of the company. Depending on the situation and the country, getting a work visa can be relatively painless for the sponsoring company, or it can be a long, arduous and expensive process with an uncertain outcome. In many cases, the company also has to prove that the job you are doing cannot be done by a local employee (and, therefore, shows that a foreigner is not taking a job away from a local citizen).

Trying to get hired in a country where you have no work authorization creates a double whammy – you must be valuable enough for the employer to want to hire you and to want to sponsor you.

Most work visas are company specific – for example, a company might agree to hire you and sponsor you for the work visa, and that work visa then becomes specific only to that company. If you lose your job or want to work at another company, your work permit is not transferable and you must start the process all over again.

The exception are Work Exchange Visas. These exchange and reciprocity programs offer short-term general employment visas that are not employer-specific. They are for a short amount of time and only available in a few countries.

Finally, if you are a citizen of the country, you do not need a work permit. While most of us have only one nationality, many nations (including the United States) allow people to hold dual or even triple nationality. It's a long shot, but you may want to check out the countries where your parents or grandparents were born to see if you can also become a citizen of that country (and therefore able to work legally). For example, it is relatively easy to obtain Irish citizenship if you have a parent or grandparent born in the country.

How to get a work visa

The easiest way to get a work visa is to get hired by a company that has agreed to sponsor you for the work authorization. If the company you want to work for agrees to sponsor you, then you will be required to provide certain documents, such as certified copies of birth certificates, diplomas, your passports and photographs. The company will then take care of everything, and if all goes well, you will receive the visa stamped in your passport that lists the dates you are eligible to work in the country.

Unfortunately for many people, it's not that easy. Even some large companies have difficulty procuring work visas for foreign nationals, or have internal bureaucracy or policies that make it almost impossible to hire new employees without pre-existing work authorization.

Bureaucracy can be a major hurdle. Says a frustrated recruiter for a major pharmaceutical company: "We're set up so that international hiring is completely separate from domestic, and we have a company-wide policy of only hiring individuals with existing work authorization for the country in question. We don't sponsor work visas. So – please don't send me your resume if you don't have the required work authorization! It doesn't matter if you're a rocket scientist or how unique your background is, it's just very hard for us to make exceptions."

If a company doesn't hire you before you go, and therefore you don't have a work visa, you can look for a job while on a tourist visa (more on this later). A word of caution, though: Be very upfront with any potential employers about your lack of work authorization and your need to be sponsored. Branch offices of global companies with strict policies might have their hands tied even if you approach them locally. Or a company might lack the resources to sponsor you. Some companies, such as English language schools, will typically have an easier time hiring you, as they habitually hire relatively large numbers of foreigners.

If you are hired by a company in country, you will have to leave the country in order to convert your tourist visa to a working visa. Usually, a quick trip across the closest border is all that is required. You may have to bring your documents to the embassy in question, and wait a few days before re-entering the country. In most cases, your sponsoring employer should foot the bill for the trip.

Leaving the country is also necessary if you need to extend your working visa – most visas are only issued for three years or less. If you need to continue with your employer, you may have to re-enter the country in order to get the extension.

Working illegally

Working illegally, though not something to be encouraged, is certainly a fact of life for many foreigners working internationally. The most common type of illegal activity for foreigners working abroad is giving private English lessons – while a language institute may sponsor you for a work visa, in your free time you may tutor privately. This is illegal, though very common.

Other common types of illegal activity or under the table work would be casual work, like restaurant or bar work, or seasonal agricultural work. In this case, it is not worth the time or expense for the employer to sponsor legal workers, so they may be tempted to hire individuals without work authorization.

Finally, freelancing like editing, writing, acting or modeling is also technically illegal if not covered by your work permit or student visa.

Of course, most countries are much more concerned about floods of immigrants from unstable countries than they are about a few (relatively) rich Westerners coming to teach English or work in local pubs. But nonetheless, be prepared for the worst case scenario – deportation – if you decide to go this route.

Deportation means being forced to leave the country, sometimes at an hours' notice, and then being barred from the country for a period of time, sometimes for life.

Visit Vault at **www.vault.com** for insider company profiles, expert advice, career message boards, expert resume reviews, the Vault Job Board and more.

VAULT CAREER LIBRARY   85

Student visas vs. tourist visas

Most student visas are valid only for the courses and/or institute outlined on the original application for the visa. Getting a student visa is generally easier than getting a work permit, but bear in mind that student visas do not allow you to work. So even if you are only studying for a few hours a day, and have plenty of free time for teaching or editing, if you are caught working, you may be deported.

Nonetheless, student visas can be an attractive alternative to tourist visas if you are intent on working illegally: They are generally for a longer period of time (up to 12 months) and arouse less suspicion at the airport or when leaving and re-entering the country. The downside, of course, is the fact that you have to pay tuition and go to class!

Be careful

A company must be legally incorporated in order to sponsor an employee legally. While this may sound very intuitive, be careful! Make sure the company sponsoring you is actually a company, and that your work visa and working papers are not forged. A recent scam in Russia involved unregistered language academies illegally hiring foreign teachers. When the school was shut down, the teachers also faced deportation – even though they thought their work visas were valid and in order.

Also be wary of country quirks; for example, in the Czech Republic, a work permit must be accompanied by a resident's permit. Unless you have both, you are not considered to be legally working in the country.

Finally, don't mess around with visas and work authorization. Don't overstay your welcome. If you are unclear about anything, contact your embassy for more information.

Preparations

Before you go, there are many practical considerations involved in relocation that you need to think about. Depending on your situation, you may be more or less on your own for the following items. If you are studying abroad, or being transferred by your company, you may have a lot of the following items taken care of for you. If you're going alone, you'll have a lot on your plate. Nonetheless, check out each one, and if in doubt about who is responsible, make sure you check with your employer or your school.

Being aware of what you take into account when moving overseas will also help you plan your budget.

The move

When thinking about moving overseas, you need to decide how much of your personal possessions you will bring, and how much you need to bring. When deciding, consider the following:

• Is accommodation provided for me? Is it furnished or unfurnished?

• Where will I be staying?

• Can I easily buy everything I need once I get there?

• Am I returning to my current apartment?

Once you've decided how much stuff you're bringing and how much you're leaving, you should compare the costs of moving, storing or selling your belongings. Estimate the cost of the move, including buying replacing furniture and selling anything you might decide to. Check out www.homestore.com for a calculator to help you estimate the cost of moving.

Passport and visas

If you don't have a current passport, you'll need to get one before you travel overseas. If you have a passport but it is full of stamps or within 12 months of its expiry date, you should get a new one before leaving the U.S. Many countries will not give you a visa if there is no place to put the stamp, or if your passport is set to expire soon.

If you're pressed for time, you may consider using a passport expediting service which can speed up the renewal process. Check out

Visit Vault at **www.vault.com** for insider company profiles, expert advice, career message boards, expert resume reviews, the Vault Job Board and more.

V**A**ULT CAREER LIBRARY   **87**

www.passportsandvisas.com. These services can be costly, though, so if you've got the time, apply directly.

If you are entering on a tourist visa, you may need to apply for that before you go. Some tourist visas also cost money, so make sure you know the details and the cost before you go.

Health insurance

This is one thing you don't want to leave home without. Get it, and make sure it's active from the time the plane takes off. Don't wait to arrive at your destination before you look for insurance.

If you are working and already have a job, your company will probably have taken care of insurance for you (make sure you check the details of the coverage). If you're looking for a job, consider taking out health insurance yourself, for a few months or even a year. Make sure the insurance you take out is extendable if necessary. Check out the following sources for information and quotes:

www.intlhealthinsurance.com – International Health Insurance, offers policies for short-term and long-term stays abroad.

www.internationalstudentinsurance.com – For students only, part of the Internationalstudent.com network.

Also check out the www.state.gov site for information on what type of vaccinations you might need, and some tips and resources for medical issues abroad.

Vaccinations

You may need vaccinations for such diseases as typhus, cholera and malaria if your destination is outside of Western Europe. Use the Centers for Disease Control web site (www.cdc.gov/travel) or the World Health Organization web site (www) to determine if you need vaccinations and how much they cost.

Be aware that some hepatitis vaccines take multiple inoculations and need to be spread out over several months, so make sure you give yourself enough time if you need this one.

Travel and airfare

The cheapest airfares are ones that are flexible in their departure dates, and don't coincide with major holidays and/or the "peak season" (generally summer and December). Use a discount travel web site or, if you qualify, check out STA Travel for the best student prices. You can also, if you meet the age requirements, apply through STA for an International Student ID that will get you discounts on travel. www.statravel.com

Your best bet is a fully flexible round trip ticket that can be easily changed with little or no penalty. A note of caution – some countries require a round trip ticket (evidence you will leave the country) before they let you in as a tourist.

Accommodations

If you won't be staying with a friend, or living in company housing, one of the most pressing issues that you need to consider is where you will stay initially. This is separate from finding long-term accommodations, which may happen days or even weeks after you arrive. First, you need to figure out where you'll go from the airport.

If you're going with a work exchange or organized visa program, they will provide you with lists of cheap potential accommodations, and you might even be able to set yourself up with an apartment or a roommate before you arrive.

If you're going in cold, you'll most likely head to a hotel. Costs can mount quickly here, of course, so find one that is as cheap as possible. A good idea is to check out backpacker's guides like the Lonely Planet (www.lp.com) for hostels or low-cost accommodations in the city you're heading to. They'll be cheap, and you'll meet a lot of people, some of whom might be the same situation as you.

Initial living expenses

Make sure you have enough money to cover expenses for at least three months after arrival. Estimate your expenses by accommodation (apartment, motel, etc) and by food and entertainment.

Make sure your source for research is geared toward living cheaply and on the economy: www.expatforum.com, for example, has an excellent page on cost of living comparisons, but it is geared toward expatriates on company

Visit Vault at **www.vault.com** for insider company profiles, expert advice, career message boards, expert resume reviews, the Vault Job Board and more.

VAULT CAREER LIBRARY   **89**

transfers and shows countries such as China and Argentina as actually being more expensive than the United States.

Use the following list to make sure you haven't forgotten any expenses, and also to calculate how much you'll need to get there. If your work, school, or exchange organization is taking care of any of the items, just leave that line blank. Plan to bring more money than you think you'll need.

Vault Moving Abroad Calculator

What	Estimated Cost	Actual Cost (if you want to compare later!)
The move	$	
Health insurance	$	
Passport & visas	$	
Vaccinations	$	
Travel & airfare	$	
Initial accommodation	$	
3 months living	$	
	$	
Total	$	
Add 20% onto your initial total for unexpected and emergency situations.	$	
Final total	$	

GETTING HIRED

Getting Ready

When applying for jobs overseas, you must both prove your capabilities for the job and prove your interest in, and capability of, living in the country in question. In other words, you have to be able to very clearly express 1) **why you want to work in another country, and** 2) **why you can thrive there.**

In order to get a job abroad, follow these four steps:

Step 1
Create your international inventory.

Step 2
Develop your international story and positioning.

Step 3
Internationalize your resume and cover letter.

Step 4
Prepare for international interviews.

Even if you think these steps aren't applicable, give them a try – you'd be surprised how they clarify your thinking.

Visit Vault at **www.vault.com** for insider company profiles, expert advice, career message boards, expert resume reviews, the Vault Job Board and more.

VAULT CAREER LIBRARY   93

Step 1: Create an "International Inventory"

Step 1
Create your international inventory.

Step 2
Develop your international story and positioning.

Step 3
Internationalize your resume and cover letter.

Step 4
Prepare for international interviews.

The first step is to make a list of all your international experiences, regardless of their relevance to your job search. This

1)   Gives you confidence about your ability to work outside your home country
2)   Helps you position your experience for interviews

This first step forces you to think about your experiences and qualifications and decide how they are applicable to the work you want to do. Think of this as an "International Inventory" – you're looking for all the experiences and skills that will help position you effectively to go abroad.

Your prior experiences can be roughly divided into three categories:

1)   Previous international experience
2)   Domestic experiences and skills that are relevant to an international career
3)   Personality traits that will help you thrive outside your home country

1) Previous international experiences

The first stop in creating your International Inventory is to look at your previous international work experience. List each international job you've held below, when you held it, what you did and what you learned in each position.

Sample Vault International Inventory

Where	Doing What?	How Long?	Learnings / Skills Developed
Getting Ready	Summer exchange in high school	3 months	Basic German language skills, exposure to another culture

If you have no prior international work experience, consider other international experiences you've had. Did you live abroad as a child? Did you do an exchange semester or summer at college? Have you backpacked through Europe? Don't overlook any experience, no matter how trifling you might think it is.

Finally, look at your travel experience. If you have extended periods of travel under your belt, or have spent considerable time in one part of the world, write it down. (You can leave out your trip across the border to Tijuana.)

Also look at any experiences you might have had while traveling that could help build your International Inventory. What challenges have you faced while traveling?

International Inventory Worksheet – Previous International Experiences.

Where	Doing What?	How Long?	Skills Developed

Visit Vault at www.vault.com for insider company profiles, expert advice, career message boards, expert resume reviews, the Vault Job Board and more.

VAULT CAREER LIBRARY   95

2)   Relevant domestic experiences and skills

It's now time to turn your sights on other areas of your life that have an international component. For this part of your Inventory, think about all instances where you might have participated in anything, albeit in your home country, that had an international focus or was in some way connected to other countries/cultures. Cast your net as wide as possible and write down any experience, no matter how small. You can always eliminate later.

Think through these major categories and see what you can come up with:

Academic – Language study

Be sure to write down any language study or skills you have. Even if you took French for a few semesters back in high school, write it down! Don't worry how useful your language ability will be in the country you plan to work in.

Academic – Courses studied in school

Think back to college What courses did you take that had an international component? In addition to any language courses, note any classes you've taken that have deepened your understanding of other cultures.

Academic – Extracurricular activities

List the organizations and clubs you have belonged to that focus on international issues.

Work

Have there been international aspects to any of your previous jobs?

Hobbies and interests

Do you have any interest in the music or literature of other countries? They go in the Inventory.

International Inventory Worksheet – Relevant Domestic Experiences and Skills.

Where	Doing What?	How Long?	Skills Developed

3)   Personality traits

The third piece of your International Inventory is a little different. Think back now to the six personality traits required to thrive when spending an extended period of time in another country.

• Open-mindedness

• Flexibility

• Ability to cope with ambiguity

• Relationship skills

• Emotional stability

• Intellectual curiosity

Consider the first three traits. Your goal now is to come up with situations and experiences that demonstrate you have these abilities. Spend some time, and think of at least three situations where you have demonstrated open-mindedness, flexibility and ability to cope with ambiguity.

International Inventory Worksheet – Personality Traits.

	Open-mindness	Flexibility	Ability to cope with ambiguity
Do I have it?			
In what situation did I demonstrate it?			
What was the outcome?			

Voila! Your International Inventory is now complete!

You now have the basic ammunition you need to create a succinct and compelling story about **why you want to work abroad**, and **why you will be successful abroad**. Now the next step is to incorporate the results of your International Inventory into an "international story" that shows why you can – and should – work internationally.

Step 2: Develop Your International Story

Step 1
Create your international inventory.

Step 2
Develop your international story and positioning.

Step 3
Internationalize your resume and cover letter.

Step 4
Prepare for international interviews.

Now that you've developed your International Inventory, it's time to answer the "10 Questions." This exercise will help you explain to others why you want to work abroad.

To get the most out of this exercise, think through every question and write out a distinct answer to each question. Answer each question as narrowly as possible. By answering all 10, a well-rounded and compelling picture of who you are, why you want to work internationally, and why you are suitable for an international position will emerge.

1. Why do you want to work abroad?

2. Why do you want to work in this country?

3. Why do you think you will be able to work in this country?

4. What have you done to demonstrate that you can thrive internationally?

5. What personality traits do you have that show you are suitable for this position?

6. How will I know what you won't go home after six months?

7. You have no prior international experience – why should I hire you?

Visit Vault at **www.vault.com** for insider company profiles, expert advice, career message boards, expert resume reviews, the Vault Job Board and more.

V/\ULT CAREER LIBRARY   **99**

8. How have you prepared for a career (in this country)?

9. What is the toughest situation you have ever worked in?

10. What is the most challenging personal situation you have ever been in ?

From the 10 Questions comes the "international story" that you'll tell to potential employers.

Step 3: Internationalize Your Resume and Cover Letter

Step 1
Create your international inventory.

Step 2
Develop your international story and positioning.

Step 3
Internationalize your resume and cover letter.

Step 4
Prepare for international interviews.

There are many resources to help you write a fantastic resume and cover letter. There are a few key things, however, that you should keep in mind while writing an internationally oriented resume and cover letter, so keep reading!

Resume

Differences

There are several key differences between a resume you might use for a job hunt in the Americas, and one that is appropriate for use outside the United States. The first difference is the terminology – you might hear the term "curriculum vitae" used to refer to non-American resumes. A curriculum vitae, or CV for short, is basically the same as a standard resume, except for one key aspect – the length.

Unlike American resumes, which are typically one page long, CVs can run to three, four or even five pages. With a CV, the emphasis is on providing in-depth information about your work experience, rather than being short and concise. Use the extra space to elaborate (in an effective manner) on experiences that might normally be omitted from a standard resume. Explain your employment in depth, and reference specific projects, responsibilities and accomplishments from your International Inventory.

CVs include much more personal information than American resumes. Overseas employers, for example, routinely request that you attach a recent photograph to your CV. Be prepared to put your age, nationality, marital status and work authorization (if any) on your CV. While much of this information would be illegal to require on an American resume, employers in many countries request that you include this information.

For more information, take a look at *The Global Resume and CV Guide* by Mary Anne Thompson. The guide provides information on resume styles for over 40 countries.

Job objective/employment goal

State clearly that you are looking for an international position, and narrow down your geographic focus as much as possible. Avoid using titles, as they might mean different things in different contexts. Here are some sample goals:

• A position in sales and market development in East Asia

• An operations position in the software industry in France

• Experienced teacher seeking ESL position in Seoul, South Korea.

Academic credentials

Add a line or two to your CV to list extracurricular activities or classes that relate to your geographic focus.

For example:

University of Michigan
Bachelor of Arts in Political Science
Courses taken include Emerging Economies of Eastern Europe and Russian language classes (intermediate level)

Visit Vault at **www.vault.com** for insider company profiles, expert advice, career message boards, expert resume reviews, the Vault Job Board and more.

VAULT CAREER LIBRARY **101**

Senior Thesis on "The Banking System in Uzbekistan"

Work experience

Focus on any jobs or customers with an international focus. Make sure you include a sentence or two to define any non-international employers.

Summer Intern, Boland Industries

A mid-sized California-based industrial electronics components manufacturer with annual revenue of $35 million

Other

If your standard resume doesn't already include a section for additional information, create it. List travel experience, extracurricular activities, volunteer activities, and anything else that supports your international orientation.

Languages

If applicable, create a separate section for languages spoken and studied.

Cover letters

- Be as formal as possible, perhaps more formal than in the U.S.

- Avoid arcane or overly academic language. The person reading the letter may not speak English as their first language

- Do not allude to events or situations that are culture-specific. When in doubt, explain all and everything in a simple, concise manner.

The cover letter is your chance to make sure all the points from your International Inventory that aren't effectively covered in your CV are properly highlighted, and that your international story is strongly and coherently expressed.

Be sure to answer, in your cover letter, why you want to work abroad, why you will be good at it, and why you want to work in the country that you are targeting. For example:

- Through past experiences I have demonstrated my ability to work in challenging, unfamiliar environments.

- While in this position, I was responsible for interfacing with our South American client base. This gave me a deep interest in and desire to pursue more in depth business in that region.

Sample Resume – Before

Matthew is a 26-year-old marketer who is planning to look for work in Latin America. This is the non-internationalized version of his resume.

Matthew Brown
555 Minetta Lane
New York, New York 11000
212-932-4555
mbrown@hotmail.com

EDUCATION

St. Martin's University, Minnesota   (Dates)
Bachelor of Arts; Major in Political Science, Minor in Spanish Language and Literature
GPA 3.55, Dean's List
- Active in debating union and volleyball team
- Elected vice president, Theta Chi Fraternity

WORK EXPERIENCE

National Household Goods Company
Assistant Brand Manager, Cleaning Products   (Dates, 2 years)
- Analyzed target verticals for consumer expansion
- Launched new cleansing product in Eastern region
- Led specialty display initiative within client stores; doubled number of displays in a 15-month period

Local Sporting Company
Marketing and Communications Intern   (Dates, 2 summers)
- Assisted in development of marketing collateral for new product launch
- Conducted focus groups and analyzed results
- Managed in-store displays during sale campaign

INTERESTS

- Latin American Literature, volleyball, volunteering

Sample Resume – After

Matthew is a 26-year-old marketer who is planning to look for work in Latin America. This is the internationalized version of his resume.

Matthew Brown
555 Minetta Lane
New York, New York 11000
212-932-4555
mbrown@hotmail.com

Matthew is looking for a job from the United States, so he is keeping his address and telephone number. If you are in transit, remove your address and telephone number altogether and just keep a valid e-mail address.

Age: 26   **Nationality:**   American

Here Matthew has added his age and his nationality.

Objective
A marketing position with a fast growing consumer products company in Latin America

Here Matthew has added an objective. He has not added a summary to his resume, since his work experience is short enough.

Work Experience

National Household Goods Company
Assistant Brand Manager, Cleaning Products   2 years

During my two years working for the Cleaning Products Department (annual turnover $1.2 billion) I worked on various assignments of increasing responsibility, including analysis of the Venezuelan and Columbian markets for possible launch of new products. During this project I coordinated and worked closely with our Latin American offices. Other activities included the successful launch of a new line of organic cleansing products and a specialty display initiative within client stores that resulted in a doubling of the number of displays over a 15-month period.

Local Sport Marketing Company – $3 million revenue specialty marketing company focused on sports and entertainment marketing.
Marketing and Communications Intern   2 summers

During the two summers that I interned at this local company, I learned the basics of marketing communication, including how to conduct focus groups, how to analyze results, and the basics of merchandizing.

Matthew has eliminated the bullet style of his previous resume and expanded his accomplishments in a paragraph style where he is able to elaborate more fully. He highlights a recent project that demonstrates Latin American work experience. For his internship work experience, Matthew adds an explanatory sentence about the company itself, and stresses the learning aspect of his internship. Latin American readers may not be familiar with college internships. (In many countries outside of North America, the "college intern" is not a common phenomena.)

EDUCATION

St. Martin's University, Minnesota
Dates
Bachelor of Arts; Major in Political Science, minor in Spanish Language and Literature
GPA 3.55 on a 4.0 scale, Dean's List (top 20% of graduating class)
• Active in debating union and volleyball team and Theta Chi fraternity (Vice President)
• Senior Thesis: "The Role of the Rising Middle Class in the Democracy Movement in Brazil"

Matthew has moved education below work experience, and added some explanatory information about his GPA and what the Dean's list means. He has consolidated his activities and allowed space to highlight his senior thesis on Latin America.

LANGUAGES

English: Native fluency
Spanish: Fluent
Portuguese: Proficient

Since his language skills are impressive (and relevant to his job search) Matthew has created a separate section to highlight them. He also indicates his mother tongue (English).

INTERESTS

• Latin American literature
• Volleyball and sports
• Volunteering – volunteered for three semesters as a crisis translator at the local church, working primarily with Central American refugees

Again, Matthew highlights the specifics of his volunteer activities that involved speaking Spanish.

Visit Vault at **www.vault.com** for insider company profiles, expert advice, career message boards, expert resume reviews, the Vault Job Board and more.

VAULT CAREER LIBRARY   **105**

Step 4: Preparing for Interviews

Step 1
Create your international inventory.

Step 2
Develop your international story and positioning.

Step 3
Internationalize your resume and cover letter.

Step 4
Prepare for international interviews.

International Interviews

In addition to answers about the specific job and the specific company you are interviewing for, you should be ready to answer all the questions from the 10 Questions. Be prepared to expand on them and elaborate with examples and situations from your International Inventory.

When you are interviewing, your challenge is to ensure you show enough enthusiasm for the job, the company and the location. Striking a balance is crucial: don't show that you are only interested in the job and imply that you are not interested in living outside your home country. On the other hand, don't let your enthusiasm for going abroad grow so strong that it appears you only care about moving.

Most companies, obviously, are reluctant to invest the time and effort to hire a potential employee who isn't interested in a long-term commitment

A Failed Interview

After working for a few years with a major accounting firm in London, Joanna decided she wanted to move on. Reluctant to return home, and interested in exploring another part of Europe, Joanna applied to management consulting companies around Europe. She blanketed the region with her resume and cover letter, applying to offices in approximately 10 different cities. She wasn't fussy about where she ended up; having enjoyed her time in England, she was confident she would be fine in any number of other countries.

She followed up on many of the resumes with telephone calls to old friends, ex-colleagues and alumni from her university in America. A few weeks into her job hunt, she received a phone call from the Milan office of a top consulting company. Joanna was all ready with her reasons why she wanted to work for the company, and with the reference from a friend who worked in the office (and who had passed along her resume to the head recruiter), but she had not thought through one crucial question. It came up within the first 10 minutes of the initial phone call: "Why Italy?"

The truth was, Joanna wasn't particularly interested in the Milan office, and was happy to go anywhere in Europe. But that was obviously not the sort of reasoning she could highlight in an interview. She remembers blustering a little and saying something general about wanting to work in Italy, but she knew the recruiter was not convinced. The phone call lasted a few minutes more, but Joanna could tell the recruiter had lost interest.

After she hung up, Joanna wanted to kick herself. "Being unprepared to answer that simple question cost me the position, or at least the chance to continue talking to them. They were interested in getting to know me, hence their phone call. But I never heard from them again.

Even if I wasn't particularly interested in Italy or Milan, I should have had a really strong answer ready. I easily could have talked about my interest in the region, the Italian clients I had worked with previously, and could have cited any number of positive experiences from people I knew that I could have said had convinced me. Unfortunately, I said none of those things and really felt like I wasted the recruiter's time!"

Visit Vault at **www.vault.com** for insider company profiles, expert advice, career message boards, expert resume reviews, the Vault Job Board and more.

VAULT CAREER LIBRARY   **107**

Cultural differences in interviewing

While it is hard to generalize across cultures, here are some tips you might want to consider when interviewing for a job, either in another country, or domestically with a foreign recruiter.

- **Formality**. Many cultures are more formal than North American culture. Do not use first names during the interview, and don't be surprised if you are addressed as Ms. or Mr. Follow all the normal rules for being respectful. Don't sit until you are asked, try not to cross your legs, and get out of your seat when the interviewer rises.

- **Neutrality**. Again, this is something that transcends cultural differences in interviewing, but is perhaps all the more important when dealing with another culture. Be as neutral as possible when talking about non-work related, and even work-related, issues. Don't show strong approval or disapproval about anything – you do not know yet what is acceptable or not acceptable culturally, so avoid stepping on any potential minefields. Avoid political comments.

- **Humor**. Humor is sometimes a great way to establish rapport with an interviewer, especially when things are going well and the timing is right. However, unless you are certain that your jokes will be considered funny, avoid humor during the interview.

Acceptable questions in an international interview

You might be asked questions about your marital status, your relationship status, your political opinions, your age and other questions that you might feel cross the line between professional and personal information.

These types of questions, obviously, are more likely to come from foreign recruiters, rather than recruiters working for American companies with offices abroad. Should you answer? While there may be exceptions, the short answer is yes. Chances are the interviewer is asking you questions that are acceptable in the country in which you would like to work.

The phone interview

You should be prepared for phone interviews. Unless you are in-country and networking locally, most remote job searches will involve some variation of the phone interview.

Phone interviews are different than face-to-face interviews, and present additional challenges that may also be exacerbated by cultural/language differences. Interviews are traditionally a way to evaluate intangibles – motivation, loyalty, enthusiasm, focus and commitment. How do you convey these traits when you are not face-to-face with the potential employer? Without the benefit of body language and physical cues, it is difficult to develop rapport with the interviewer.

So, how can you make a connection? Make a conscious effort to remain upbeat, ask good questions and use the interviewer's name whenever possible. But don't try too hard. While this may sound counterintuitive, being overly friendly and overcompensating for the lack of visual cues can often backfire. Without the visual cues, you stand a good chance of going down the wrong path.

Don't get flustered if you can't gauge the interviewer's reaction to what you are saying. Maintain your calm, and keep an even pace of talking. Above all, don't rush anything. Make an effort to speak slowly. There may be a small time lag with the phone connection. If in doubt or if you appear to be interrupting the interviewer, remain silent and wait for him to take the initiative.

Another disadvantage of the phone interview is that you never know when it might occur. Unless you have scheduled the interview ahead of time you run the risk of being caught flatfooted.

Tips for surviving a phone interview

• Be prepared: Have your answers ready and written down if possible. One advantage of a phone interview compared to an in-person interview is you can have notes in front of you. You should avoid sounding rehearsed or as though you're reading, but do take advantage of this aspect of the phone interview to have as many "props" as you need.

• Write down answers and take notes as you're talking and listening.

• Try to anticipate any follow-up questions the interviewer might ask.

• Be clear and succinct. Don't ramble.

Visit Vault at **www.vault.com** for insider company profiles, expert advice, career message boards, expert resume reviews, the Vault Job Board and more.

V∧ULT CAREER LIBRARY   **109**

The Unexpected Phone Interview

Patrick had previous experience working in Taiwan for several years. After completing a diploma in management studies focused on Asia, he pursued opportunities in mainland China. He spoke Chinese from his childhood, and had a lot of American contacts from Taiwan who were now working in China. Because of his language skills and experience in the region, he felt comfortable directly approaching joint ventures located on the mainland.

He describes what happened next: "I received a phone call about 3 a.m. from a rather clueless HR officer based in Shanghai. She had obviously forgotten about the time difference with the West Coast. I didn't want to embarrass the woman, so rather than point out the mistake I tried to wake myself up. Unfortunately, the connection was bad, she had a heavy accent I couldn't really identify, and my crib sheet on the company and the position were somewhere buried in a pile of papers on my desk – not in my bedroom!"

Surprisingly, Patrick did eventually get the job on the basis of that telephone call. His advice for long distance job-seekers? "Be organized. Know who might be calling, and for what position. Have your information near you at all times. And whenever possible, arrange things so that you call them. Set the agenda yourself in order to avoid surprises."

Finding the Job

CHAPTER 7

Direct from Campus

Unfortunately for American students, most companies aren't scouring college campuses to hire students to work internationally. One exception: companies seeking foreign nationals with language and work experience who wish to return to their home countries. As one recruiter says, "Our college recruiting is driven by work authorization. It is not common for us to hire students for operations where they have no previous work and living experience. There are a few exceptions for United States citizens who have worked or lived in Europe and Japan – and have fluency in the written and spoken local languages."

But for most students, work authorization proves to be a big hurdle. Says one senior career counselor who works with undergraduates: "Finding overseas jobs, either internships or full-time positions, is getting much more difficult these days. The current crackdown on immigration and visas in the United States is paralleled by a crackdown in other countries. This is especially apparent in Europe, where traditionally most of our new graduates looking to work overseas have gone. Now, it's much more difficult and employers are more reluctant to start the process of visa sponsoring because they're not sure of the results. These days, employers want dual nationality or an existing work authorization. This can be very frustrating for students." She recommends that students determined to work abroad try to teach English or enter a trainee program, rather than directly targeting an international office immediately after graduation.

The situation for finding a job directly is a little easier after graduating from an MBA program, especially if you've gone to a prestigious school or one with a strong international focus.

Top internationally focused MBA programs:

- Thunderbird Graduate School of Management
- University of Southern California (Marshall)
- University of Pennsylvania (Wharton)
- New York University (Stern)
- Columbia Business School

Many multinational consumer and financial service companies will routinely hire top MBAs for positions outside of the United States. Says one recent MBA graduate who landed a summer internship with a bank in London (which turned into a full-time job offer): "It wasn't easy, and I had to do a lot of convincing that I was serious about the long term. Intern hires are department and office-specific, and the London desk I was talking to didn't want to 'waste' their allocation for interns on someone they knew would probably not come back. But I convinced them – I did a lot of background research and spent a lot of time on the phone with other employees in the London office – I think I persuaded them I was serious. Plus, I think it helped that I had a boyfriend living over there."

The onus is on you, the MBA, to convince international employers that you don't just want a vacation, but that you are dedicated to building a long-term, post graduation career with them in the country where you will be interning.

If you're truly interested in working abroad, we recommend you affiliate yourself with an internship program that either finds you an internship or offers you the support and resources to do so, including acquiring the all-important work visa

On-campus resources

If you've decided that you do want to target an international position after college, make sure you take full advantage of the on-campus resources your university has to offer. What is available differs on every campus, but in addition to the traditional career center, your college or university will have a center for international students and/or programs that can also offer you valuable guidance.

Services that both the career center as well as the international center may offer include:

- Lists of students previously hired for international positions that you can contact for networking purposes

- Lists of companies that have previously hired American students directly into overseas offices

- Resources and databases of companies in specific countries that you can contact directly

- Alumni resources

- Links to other resources

• Career counselors who might be able to work closely with you to target the most appropriate companies

Finally, should you even consider getting a job overseas right out of college? In some cases, having a few years of American work experience under your belt before heading off is a good idea. It will make your international job search easier, as you will have some solid work experience, and help when you return to the U.S. Says one woman who worked for two years in the United States before moving to Italy for a few years: "When I returned I definitely got the sense that my American experience was important. It proved that I was able to work in an American context. I don't think I would had had the same reaction if I had no American work experience on my resume."

Internship and Volunteer Programs

Another option for students is to work abroad via work exchange programs or volunteer programs. Often, the best time to search for jobs overseas is when you are a student or a recent graduate, due to the number of such programs available for students and recent graduates.

In The Scoop, we gave an overview of the variety of study abroad, intern abroad, and volunteer abroad programs available to students, recent grads, and individuals who have been in the work force for a while. Going with a program enables you to get your working visa more easily. The types of programs that can take you abroad include:

1. Study abroad program

2. Work exchange and visa programs

3. Volunteer programs

There are also programs for potential English teachers, but we'll cover those in the next section.

Deciding on the right program

The first step when looking at international programs is to decide what you want from your international career. Do you want a particularly kind of work experience? Must you live in a certain country? How are your language skills? What is more important for you – location or work experience? How

Visit Vault at www.vault.com for insider company profiles, expert advice, career message boards, expert resume reviews, the Vault Job Board and more.

VAULT CAREER LIBRARY   113

does it fit into your future plans? Are you prepared to work for free (or a tiny stipend)?

Once you've started to narrow down your options, use on-line directories and databases such as CIEE and IEE Passport to help you narrow down your options even further. Both have a search function that allow you to search opportunities, both full-time and internship, by location and subject.

Evaluating programs

Before you consider applying to a program, learn as much about it as possible. Research is especially true for "for profit" programs – you need to make sure they will provide a quality experience.

Programs vary greatly in what they cover and what they provide for. Make sure you seek out administrators, current students and alumni to help you answer the questions below.

Administrators

- How long has the program been in existence?

- How many volunteers/students have gone through the program?

- What percentage of participants go home early?

- (If applicable) Are internships/placements guaranteed?

- (If competitive) What makes a successful applicant?

Logistics and expenses:

- (If applicable) Is the work visa taken care of? Who pays for it?

- Is airfare included? Is it a return ticket?

- What vaccinations are required?

- Is housing provided? What type of accommodation is offered?

- Is there a stipend? If so, how much? Is tax taken out of it?

- Are there any other perks that you are not aware of? Vacation pay?

Current participants

- Why did you decide to do the program?

- What has been the best part so far?

- Are you satisfied with your experience?

- What is the main reason people are not satisfied?

- What advice would you have for me?

Alumni and recent graduates

- Overall, how would you describe your experience?

- What was the best part of your experience? The worst part?

- Knowing my situation and my goals, would you recommend I do the program?

It might take a little bit of digging to find alumni, but it's well worth the effort. Many of the larger and more established programs have online message boards for potential, current and past participants.

The application process and interviews

Some programs require a rigorous application and selection procedure. Find out whether admissions are based more on achievements or attitude. For some programs, the selection process is not based on academic achievements as much as it is on stamina and commitment to the cause.

One recruiter from the Peace Corps gives this advice to potential applicants: "The number-one most important thing you can do during the application process is to show your commitment. It's going to be a long process, and we want to make sure that you really are dedicated. For many applicants, PC is just one choice of many, and it will certainly help your chances if you can demonstrate to us that PC is not a fallback position for you, but one that you're truly dedicated to."

Make sure you leave yourself enough time to meet all the application deadlines and start working on your applications as early as possible. Don't underestimate how time consuming it can be to prepare and gather the necessary documents, including certified copies of diplomas, passports, and write your essays and gather references, etc.

Visit Vault at **www.vault.com** for insider company profiles, expert advice, career message boards, expert resume reviews, the Vault Job Board and more.

VAULT CAREER LIBRARY   115

Teaching English

There are many options if you are interested in teaching English abroad. You can choose to teach English through a government program, through a private organization or on your own.

The following chart summarizes the options:

	Examples	Suitable For	Upside	Downside
Government Programs	JET in Japan, EPIK in Korea	First-time English teachers	Structured environment; high pay	No control over where you are placed
Volunteer & Work Abroad Placements	CIEE Educational Services Int'l	First-time English teachers	Lots of structure and support; long- and short-term assignments	Lower pay, and in some cases, you must pay for the opportunity
On your own	You	TEFL qualified Those with preexisting country connections	Flexibility; potential to make money	Need to do your own quality control on schools; no support; possibly illegal

Government programs

Government programs are set up by the governments of various countries as a way to encourage Westerners to come and teach English in public schools, thus improving the spoken English fluency of the population. Teachers are typically placed in elementary, junior high and high schools (or their equivalent). Japan was the first to implement such a program, the JET program, which has been in existence for more than 30 years. South Korea has a similar program, EPIK.

These programs offer a structured experience for first-time teachers. Your visa and transportation will be arranged for you, and you will have the support of the government of the country where you're teaching. You also don't need teaching experience or knowledge of the native language

On the other hand, some first-time teachers are placed in very rural areas, which can be isolating.

Check out the following web sites for more information:

JET in Japan: www.jetprogramme.org
EPIK in Korea: www.epik.knue.ac.kr

Volunteer agencies

There are many nonprofit (and private) organizations that offer you the chance to teach English all over the world. You may also find yourself in some of the least developed nations of the world that have no homegrown English teaching industry. Some programs offer TESL training, which can be a nice bonus.

While some volunteer agencies offer you a stipend, others require you to pay to teach. You may also be placed in an area that's not to your liking.

The following is just a sample of the many opportunities to teach as a volunteer:

- **www.ciee.org:** In addition to study and work abroad programs, the CIEE also offers volunteer teaching g programs. Currently offers programs in China and Thailand.

- **www.globalvolunteers.org:** Offers structured volunteer teaching opportunities in 12 countries.

- **www.i-to-i.com:** Variety of volunteer placements, including many for teaching English.

- **www.culturalembrace.com:** Private organization offering teaching opportunities in six countries.

Private school

It is entirely possible to find a position teaching English in another country without ever leaving home. There are a host of web sites that focus on international English teaching positions. Many offer everything from job listings to travel insurance to TEFL certificates. One English teacher now based in Prague says there's no reason to travel to another country without an English teaching job, if that's your goal. "There are so many postings on the Internet, you should be able to secure something before you arrive."

Visit Vault at **www.vault.com** for insider company profiles, expert advice, career message boards, expert resume reviews, the Vault Job Board and more.

VAULT CAREER LIBRARY   **117**

Teaching English Resources

Check out these web sites for resources on teaching English and TEFL certificates and job openings:

General:

www.eslcafe.com: Dave's ESL Café, the one, the only, the original ESL job board and community group. Enormous amount of information and great peer-to-peer dialogues on every question and every region imaginable. Some job postings get more than 5,000 hits, so be aware if you're applying to some of the more popular jobs on this site: your application could get bounced back (or at least lost in the pile!).

www.teachabroad.com: Another web site form the GoAbroad.com network, offers an extensive directory of teaching jobs and positions. Schools post job openings directly on the site.

www.tefl.com: Extensive job board. Brit-focused. Also offers you the opportunity to post your own resume during your search.

www.teachers.net: Lots of resources, including a job board, but probably better for after you get the job. Lesson plans, game ideas, and lots of teaching tips.

www.eslfocus.com: Articles and resources for teachers.

How easy is it to get hired directly by a school? It depends on the location and the desirability of the position and your background and experience. But it's safe to say that if you are serious about teaching English abroad, you can get a job remotely. A school in a remote area of Indonesia says: "We regularly use job posting sites for our recruitment. Otherwise, we wouldn't be able to get teachers. We can't interview them – sure we'd prefer if they were on the ground, but we have found remote applications to work well for us." Another school in Prague reported that 34 of the 40 teachers it hired in 2003 were hired through online job boards.

If you are applying to a job posting on one of the more popular ESL job hunting web sites, you may be one of hundreds, even thousands, applying for an attractive position. One frustrated ESL job seeker complained of application e-mails bouncing back because schools' mailboxes fill up quickly. A school director cautions, "The job site we post on causes a huge rush of resumes. So if you do apply, make sure your resume stands out. We do look for the TEFL certificate, because it shows us the applicant is serious about teaching and wants to do it for at least a few years."

So how do you make your resume stand out? Follow these tips:

- **Highlight those qualifications that make you desirable.** Spotlight your university degree, your TEFL certificate and prior teaching experience. Prior teaching experience doesn't have to be ESL-related to be impressive.

- **Make it short and succinct.** Write your cover letter in the body of your email, or include it in the same attachment as your resume (the first page). Highlight immediately why you think you would make a good teacher, and why you are interested in that particular city and/or school.

- **Clearly give contact numbers.** Provide both phone and e-mail, and indicate when you are available for a phone interview.

- **Try and give the school a sense of who you are.** One of the key aspects of a successful teacher is the ability to interact with students. Demonstrate you are a people person and let your personality shine through.

Rather than applying directly yourself, you can also consider using a "placement agency." These agencies exist primarily in Korea and Japan. They are paid by schools in these countries to recruit teachers. The agent shops your resume, finds you a position and gets you the work visa (in conjunction with your destination school). Often, you don't have to pay for this service, as they are normally paid by the schools they are recruiting for. If you do have to pay a fee, make sure you know what you are paying for and feel comfortable with the arrangement.

Says the owner of one placement agency that specializes in Korean placements: "A good reason to deal with us is that we will get you a reliable school, and you will have someone to help you during your contract if you need it." Often, the schools agencies represent are in remote areas that have trouble attracting applicants.

If you are looking for an English teaching job independently, sometimes the most effective way to find a position is to travel to your target country on a tourist visa and shop around. There are advantages to taking this route. For one, you can check out potential employers and institutions in person, even speak to potential coworkers. (If you are hired, you will have to leave the country and reenter to receive your work visa; a tourist visa cannot be upgraded in country.)

Visit Vault at **www.vault.com** for insider company profiles, expert advice, career message boards, expert resume reviews, the Vault Job Board and more.

VAULT CAREER LIBRARY   **119**

If you're going this route, choose a destination that has a large and thriving English teaching community. Jobs will be plentiful, and there will also be plenty of other teachers around to give you advice, support and job leads. Countries like the Czech Republic, Turkey, Hungary, Japan, Korea, Taiwan, China and Russia are your best bets if you are going to show up and look for work.

Check out the Job Information Journal on Dave's ESL Café at www.eslcafe.com. You can use this resource to search by country and region, and find out advice, tips and school information from current and prior teachers.

Evaluating schools

If you're applying to a job via the Internet, there is obviously some risk involved. How can you evaluate the school and how it treats its teachers?

As you're thinking about accepting an offer remotely, use this checklist to help you make sure you understand exactly what you're going into.

Checklist to evaluate schools

- How long has the school been in existence?

- How many teachers does the school currently have?

- How many teachers don't finish their contract? Why?

- Who pays for the work visa? How long does it usually take?

- What is the salary? What is the tax rate?

- Does the school provide a free round-trip ticket or at least pay for a ticket home?

- How many vacation days are included?

- Is health insurance included? Are there any paid sick days?

- Is housing included?

- Does the school give a bonus for successful contract completion?

To TEFL or not to TEFL?

Should you get your TEFL certificate (or a variation thereof)? The answer: it depends. While the TEFL is always a plus, it's not always a requirement.

Typically, the TEFL is more of an asset when applying to more "established" institutions, such as colleges, or when looking for jobs in a more crowded market, like Kyoto in Japan. It's also a big plus if you wish to find a job online before arriving in country. It's not needed if you intend to work at smaller language schools or in countries where the demand for English teachers far exceeds the supply. Government-run programs like JET and EPIK have no TEFL requirement at all.

In short, whether you should get a TEFL or equivalent certificate depends on a variety of considerations, including:

- Your long-term commitment to a career as a teacher

- Your choice of geographic location

- If you have prior teaching experience

- If you are participating in a program that requires it

- Your own personal confidence (first-time teaching can be very daunting!)

- Whether you are applying in country or from your home country

There are a large number of schools offering the certificate – and a large number of disreputable schools, too. If you have made the decision to do the course, make sure you do your homework first. Paying for a TEFL is an investment, and before you commit to a course, make sure you will be getting what you are paying for, which should be qualified instructors, decent accommodation and help finding jobs after the program is over.

Checklist for evaluating TEFL programs:

- Make sure that teachers are qualified

- Investigate the school's track record of graduates and job placements

- Determine what is included and not included in the cost of the course

- Find out what kind of housing is offered

- Find out whether the program offers classroom training.

Visit Vault at **www.vault.com** for insider company profiles, expert advice, career message boards, expert resume reviews, the Vault Job Board and more.

VAULT CAREER LIBRARY   121

Company Transfer

Getting a corporate transfer is in many ways the ideal way to go abroad, assuming you like the company you're working for. You are placed into a working environment that will be at least somewhat familiar to you, the logistics – and often the expense – of moving and relocating are taken care of for you, and the work visa is a non-issue.

The two best ways to win an international transfer are to work for a company that has a standard management trainee program with an international rotation, or to work for a company that has many offices around the world and regularly transfers employees between offices.

These steps can help you ease your corporate transfer.

Step #1: Do your homework

Choose your office. Be realistic about expectations for working in another office, and what you can bring to the table. Find out what language is spoken in the office and if foreign language proficiency is necessary.

Take into consideration the type of work you do; anything involved in sales or HR will usually require a good command of the local language, whereas a function like finance might have less need for top language skills.

Step #2: Make your intentions known

Be upfront about your intentions. Engage your boss and co-workers and talk with them realistically and frankly about your desires, your reasons and your motivations for an international transfer. Frame your desire to work abroad in terms of your future at the firm, not your need for novelty.

Step #3: Be flexible

Be sensitive to the needs of your employer. For example, if you're targeting a sales position overseas similar to your current job, but then discover that the sales forces is set up very differently in your target office, you might need to modify your goals. Be prepared to be flexible with your goals, even your career path, in order to land an overseas position.

If your company does not transfer you, you must think seriously about whether you wish to remain with your company. If you have decided to leave your employer if you cannot transfer offices, then inform your supervisor of this fact. But don't do this if you don't intend to leave your job – you may find your bluff called!

Networking effectively

Rely on the HR department for formal job openings, and to help guide you about company relocation, transfer policies and salary guidelines. Don't rely on them to get you a job. The best way to transfer internationally, barring an official transfer or rotation program, is to network internally.

Use this list of people to help you develop your target network list:

• All employees in the department you'd like to work in

• All foreigners in the office in the country you'd like to work in

• Your potential bosses

• Those who have transferred to an international office and returned.

Hayley: A Corporate Transfer

Hayley was working in San Francisco for a company that develops software for the media industry. After working with them for a little over two years, she began to get itchy feet. "I had been in San Francisco since college, and after traveling a lot as a student, I knew I wanted to be overseas again. I had a lot of friends in San Francisco, but I was ready for adventure." Not sure of her options, Hayley explored various jobs and destinations, and talked to a couple of people. "But the biggest problem, or issue, was that I liked the company I was already working for, and I liked the industry. It was a pretty young company, the atmosphere was great, and I loved the people I was working for."

Her company had recently targeted the Asian market, and had expanded to Singapore with a branch office. The company was already established in Europe, so it wasn't their first international foray. "I decided to talk to my boss about working at the new office in Singapore." Her boss was initially supportive, but suggested she contact Curt, the head of the office in Singapore, directly. Hayley had briefly worked with Curt before his transfer and so she started e-mailing him and phoning him in Singapore.

Visit Vault at **www.vault.com** for insider company profiles, expert advice, career message boards, expert resume reviews, the Vault Job Board and more.

V∧ULT CAREER LIBRARY   **123**

"I knew the sales projections for Asia were very positive, so I guessed they were going to need to hire more people." Her assumption was correct, but apart from Curt, all plans were to hire locals with knowledge of the market and the Asian region. Hayley discovered this during her initial conversations with Curt. Undeterred, she independently created a job description and a plan that she felt would use her skills and benefit the office.

But when she brought the plan to her boss and Curt, they were still not convinced. "I felt they were stonewalling me. I knew there was no compelling reason to transfer me, and I also knew I was still needed in the San Francisco office. Even though my boss was outwardly supportive, I doubted he was behind me 100 percent, and I didn't believe them when they said they were 'considering it.'"

Hayley then decided to give an ultimatum and leave the company if they could not give her a transfer. A friend had invited her to visit Australia, and she decided, if the job would not materialize, to take a few months off and spend some time in Australia. Her plan was then to travel back through Asia and do an independent job search. When Hayley told her boss about her decision, he was quite upset and promised to keep working on her transfer. Hayley followed through on her ultimatum and left the company.

A few weeks later in Australia she received an e-mail from Curt in Singapore, asking if she was still interested in joining them. She called him from Australia, and they had a successful phone interview. Three weeks later she flew to Singapore to start working. "In the end, the ultimatum worked! I don't know if I would recommend it to everyone, but I'm glad I did it. It showed that I was serious about moving. In the end, of course, it wasn't the most convenient way to move there – I had only imagined being out of the States for a month or two – but it all worked out."

Job Hunting Before You Go

Why go this route?

Getting a job from the comfort of your own home, via the Internet or your own networking efforts, seems like a fine idea to many. The attraction of going this route is that it is less risky from a financial perspective. You don't have to budget for a job search in a foreign country, and you can look for work without incurring the expense of uprooting yourself.

However, there are some definite drawbacks to being an armchair job seeker, not the least of which is that it is very difficult to do. This route is easiest for those who are specifically skilled in an in-demand area (engineering, computers, technology) and have a definite idea of where they want to work.

While finding a job from your home country requires less upfront capital, it is nonetheless very risky from another perspective – you have less knowledge about what you are getting into. You must often sign a contract without meeting your co-workers or investigating the work site.

As discussed previously, to work legally you need to be sponsored for a work visa. This involves considerable time and expense on the part of the employer.

The three major tools for your job hunt are:

1. Online resources

2. Headhunters

3. Networking

A Note on Contracts

Employment contracts mean different things in different countries – in some, they are essentially meaningless, and the fact that you have a "contract" doesn't mean what it might in America. A contract may not even be legally enforceable. But in other countries, a "contract" might be used against you and presented as something unbreakable that might trap you against your will. Make sure you've read the fine print and understand the cultural context in which the contract is being written. If in doubt, contact the local embassy and ask for their advice.

Visit Vault at www.vault.com for insider company profiles, expert advice, career message boards, expert resume reviews, the Vault Job Board and more.

VAULT CAREER LIBRARY   125

Online resources

Below are lists of some of the larger job hunting web sites, breaking them out by those that are more generally focused versus those that concentrate primarily on international jobs. Nonetheless, many of the major domestically focused sites have significant international postings; on Monster.com, for example, almost 20 percent of the jobs listed are for international positions.

General/Domestic Focus

- www.careerbuilder.com
- www.careercast.com
- www.careerweb.com
- www.collegejournal.com
- www.employmentguide.com
- www.monster.com
- www.msncareers.com
- www.vault.com

Internationally Focused

- workabroad.monster.com. Section on the job search behemoth devoted to international jobs, with useful articles and a Q & A chatroom.
- www.escapeartist.com. "How to escape from America." Jobs, real estate and investment advice for moving abroad. An interesting slant on a common topic.
- www.expatsdirect.com. U.K.-based. Focused on executive and technical positions
- www.globalcareercenter.com. With jobs in almost 60 countries, this is one of the largest general international job boards on the Web.
- www.idealist.org. Focused on development and nonprofit work. Opportunity to post and browse short-term and long-term positions.
- www.jobsabroad.com. Part of the GoAbroad network, huge directory with all manner of international assignments.
- www.oneworld.net Focuses on development and nonprofit job postings, some very senior level.

You can also go directly to the job boards for the country in question. You'll need to be able to read the local language, of course, but these sites can be a great way to find jobs. For example, there are 21 "local" Monster sites outside of the United States. Looking for a job in Germany? Check out www.monster.de.

Additional reading

There are also several published guides that can come in handy if you're serious about using the Internet for your job hunt:

- *International Job Finder* by Daniel Lauber – a comprehensive directory of all international job web sites. Not all are equally useful, though. For example, are you really interested in the web site for mining jobs in Croatia?

- *Job Hunting on the Internet* by Richard Nelson Bolles – by the venerable author of *What Color is Your parachute?*

Company research using the Internet

You can use the Internet not only for job listing sites, but also to research the companies you are interested in. Most company web sites have a careers section through which you can apply, and they also should have contact information for global offices and branch locations. You can then use this information to contact the companies directly in the country you are considering heading to.

There are other resources for company research on the Web, too. Use the company profiles and employee surveys on www.vault.com to get background information about potential employers and the inside scoop on workplace culture and the hiring process. Hoovers.com maintains an extensive database of business information on thousands of potential employers.

Visit Vault at **www.vault.com** for insider company profiles, expert advice, career message boards, expert resume reviews, the Vault Job Board and more.

VAULT CAREER LIBRARY   **127**

Tips for Job Hunting via the Internet

Tip #1: Be specific

It's easy to be tempted to send your resume to every posting in sight. Don't. Online job posters are literally inundated with applications, and so in order to be effective, you need to follow up on every resume you send, just as you would with a regular job hunt.

Tip #2: Don't rely solely on the Internet

Be prepared to do a lot of networking and research on your own. A job search is never a passive process, and while the Internet can be a terrific source to identify jobs and submit your resume to potential employers, it is only a starting point.

Using Headhunters and Recruiting Agencies

Another tool for you to consider in your job hunt are executive recruiters, also called headhunters. Don't be put off by the title "executive recruiter" – not all recruiters concentrate on higher end positions that you might not be qualified for. It is possible to find headhunters who are both focused on filling international positions and willing to work with more junior employees.

Working with a headhunter can be a very effective and targeted way of accessing jobs remotely, especially if you have specific qualifications and skills.

Types of headhunters and recruiting agencies

Do not work with agencies that charge you a fee to find you a job. It is very hard to get any sort of guarantee that anything is going to happen with your resume once you have paid their fee.

Most headhunters are paid by the company that retains them to fill a certain position. Therefore, the cost to you as a potential applicant should be zero. But unless you fit the profile of a job the recruiter is currently seeking to fill, they won't pay much attention to you.

Placement agencies range from large employment and temporary staffing agencies to very small, exclusive boutiques employing a couple of headhunters that work in very targeted niche fields (some firms, for example, only fill positions in the medical imaging field). If you have a specific area of expertise, find a niche player. If you are more junior, and more flexible with your background and future industry, look for generalists.

Use the Internet to find placement agencies. Call or e-mail them to see what services they offer and whether they would be a good match with your situation. You may, based on their initial reply, send your resume also. Any time spent on the phone will be useful. Not only will you connect with the recruiter, you may also be able to score some job searching tips for the particular market.

There are very few recruiting agencies based in North America that specialize in placing Americans overseas. In England, however, the situation is somewhat different.

Visit Vault at **www.vault.com** for insider company profiles, expert advice, career message boards, expert resume reviews, the Vault Job Board and more.

V**A**ULT CAREER LIBRARY   **129**

The Polish branch of one British-based headhunter advises: "We usually place Polish locals in management and specialist positions. However, we do accept resumes from non-Polish nationals looking for work in Poland and other Eastern European countries. But initially, we recommend you contact personnel companies in London who specialize in job opportunities for Central and Eastern Europe and look for foreigners, mainly, not locals."

How to use this resource effectively

First, be realistic about what you will get from using a headhunter. Don't expect the world from them. The most important thing to do to use a recruiter effectively is to treat them like a potential employer. Don't expect to send your resume off and get a job easily. Remember that good recruiters get hundreds of unsolicited resumes every day. To make yours stand out from the crowd, you need to treat headhunters like potential employers – follow up and network with them after they've received your CV!

Finally, don't be discouraged if you do not get a positive reception from all recruiters you contact; you might not fit their focus.

Networking from Afar

In addition to using the Internet and internationally focused headhunters, you need to network effectively in order to find a job remotely. Often the best jobs are found through word of mouth.

How to network effectively

You need to be very focused and strategic in order to network effectively. At a bare minimum, decide which country you want to work in before networking. If you don't have a definite target country, don't squander the patience and time of your contacts yet.

Once you know where you're heading, draw up a list of potential "networkees" and divide your list of contacts into these different categories:

A. People I know well

B. People I know, but not that well

C. People I want to know

Your list will look something like this:

A. People I know well and who want to help me

Here is where you list close personal friends, relatives, and close friends of your family that might be living near or in the city of your choice. This is your A List, and the more people you have on it, the greater the chances of success.

The people on the A List are those you can ask stupid questions of, and rely on to really help you get started. They won't mind spending time with you on e-mail or the phone, answering your questions, and pointing you in the right direction. Rely on this group to give you more contacts and help you develop your strategy.

B. People I know, but not that well

Tap casual acquaintances and onetime friends. Old classmates, professors, co-workers, distant relatives, friends of friends – list them all! But don't approach your B list until you've tapped out the A list. And don't waste their time – don't approach B list contacts until you know what information you need from them.

C. People I want to know

The C list consists of contacts of contacts. Your C List should also grow every time you talk to someone on your other "lists." Follow the cardinal rule of networking: Every time you communicate with someone, don't hang up before you've got at least one name of someone else you can contact. You can also approach people directly if you find their names on web sites or in publications. As long as you have a solid reason for approaching them, they will likely be receptive enough to give you a few minutes of their time and advice.

Visit Vault at **www.vault.com** for insider company profiles, expert advice, career message boards, expert resume reviews, the Vault Job Board and more.

V/\ULT CAREER LIBRARY   **131**

Find your C listers on:

- Web sites, including destination portals, tourism sites, local job boards, local expat portals, and company web sites

- University associations

Tips for Effective Networking

If you're looking for a job at a distance, much of your networking will be done via e-mail or over the phone. You will make many cold calls and send many blind e-mails.

When making any type of networking call, make sure that you are:

1). very upfront about what you want and why you are calling; and

2). extremely mindful of their time.

Remember that when you are networking that you are using a prime resource of other people: their time. Use that time wisely. Don't ask questions you can easily get answered via a company web site or brochure.

Before making any call, prepare! Your contact will most likely not appreciate getting a call about working in Vietnam if it becomes obvious that you don't know the difference between Hanoi and Saigon.

Making cold calls to people you don't know very well can be intimidating. Consider using e-mail, especially for people you don't know or for whom you have no referral. E-mail is less intrusive and aggressive than a phone call, and allows the person receiving the note to help you on their time. Craft a short, but succinct e-mail that captures in a clear manner who you are, what you want and why you would appreciate hearing from them.

Just Going

This section has tips and advice for going to the country of your choice before you have a job.

Why go this route?

Michelle describes her experience trying to get a job in Russia while she was working in Washington, D.C.: "I spent countless hours on the phone, send tons of resumes, networked as hard as I could, and even made a two-week trip to Moscow for interviews and informational sessions. But no luck! I really sensed employers were reluctant to extend a job offer if they weren't even sure I was coming. Finally, someone gave me the best piece of advice: He said if I was serious, I should just pack up and go."

Showing up in a country and networking and job hunting locally is the best way to find unadvertised jobs. Being in the country in question, of course, also helps your networking and gives you a better sense for where and what the opportunities are. Chances are that most available jobs are not going to be advertised internationally online. In fact, it's even estimated that 80 percent of all job openings are not advertised at all!

Of course, traveling to find a job has its pitfalls. On an emotional level, going into a new country without a job can be stressful. Traveling without a job in hand can be financially tricky as well. You must have a minimum of three months of living expenses saved up; six is better. Imagine everything going wrong and how you will be able to handle that.

Know your potential salary. You won't enjoy a juicy "expat package" if you're hired in country. Even the international offices of companies from your home country will probably not offer you the same compensation as if you'd been transferred from headquarters. They may even be forced, depending on their internal bureaucracy, to offer you local wages. While local wages can certainly be livable, it's uncomfortable to be working alongside fellow Americans from corporate headquarters who are making salaries that are multiples of what you are earning.

Job hunting from your target country has the inverse risk profile of searching from home. Financially, it can be more of a burden, but in terms of being able to evaluate your potential position, your risk is less. You will be able to evaluate the companies and positions firsthand. (This dynamic is shown on the chart on the next page.)

Visit Vault at **www.vault.com** for insider company profiles, expert advice, career message boards, expert resume reviews, the Vault Job Board and more.

VAULT CAREER LIBRARY   133

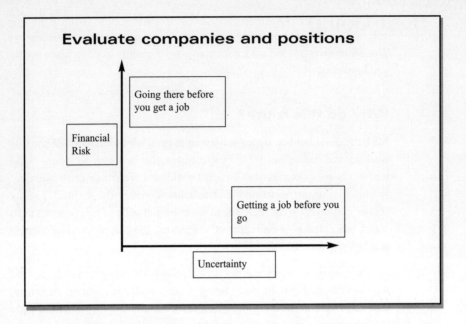

Touching down

Plan your arrival carefully. Try not to turn up during, or just before, a major holiday. Sometimes the "holiday season" can extend dramatically – in China for example, many foreigners leave in December for Christmas and the New Year. Chinese New Year falls a month or so later, so the entire three-month period from December to the end of February can be a bad time to look for a job. Likewise, many major European cities virtually shut down in August.

Arriving on a tourist visa

After you have your plane ticket, your money, and a place to stay, you will need a tourist visa. In this case, you are entering the country as a tourist and will take advantage of the 90- to 180-day period to look for work. Once you find a company to hire you, they will sponsor you and you will have to leave the country and re-enter on a working visa.

The good news about tourist visas is that they are easy to come by. American citizens usually automatically get a tourist visa upon arrival at the airport. The bad news is that some countries watch "tourists" carefully to make sure they will not be job hunting or working under the table.

Make sure you know exactly what your destination requires for a tourist visa. How long will it be issued for? Can you get an extension? Do you have to leave the country in order to get an extension? Do you have to apply for the visa before arriving at the airport? How much does getting there cost? Can you enter as a tourist with only a one-way ticket? Some countries are wary of foreigners arriving to look for jobs on tourist visas. South Korea, for example, does not allow one-way tickets for tourist visas (you'll be turned back at the airport) and might deny entry to any "tourists" they feel might be on a job hunt.

If you think you might run into problems, try to find someone who has been in the same situation and get advice. Don't trust travel agents about visas – contact embassies or consulates.

Some tourist visa regulations

Country	Visa
China	Visa required before arrival. A single and double entry China visa is good for 90 days from issuance.
England	Tourist visa granted at the airport for a stay of up to 180 days
Japan	Tourist visa granted at the airport for a stay of up to 90 days
Korea	Tourist visa granted at the airport for a stay of up to 30 days
Brazil	Tourist visas are valid for multiple entries for five years from the date issued.
France	Tourist visa granted at the airport for a stay of up to 90 days
Mexico	Tourist visa granted at the airport for a stay of up to 90 days
Russia	Visa required, valid for the exact period of your stay, and requires an in country "sponsor."

Networking tips

Once you've successfully arrived, it's time to start pounding the pavement. The following section contains tips for networking and resources to help you find a job while living overseas.

You should already have a list of people to contact. Make sure you have all their contact information with you in a paper format – you never know how long it will be before you get yourself set up with a proper Internet connection (or even a convenient, working phone).

The other foreigners on the ground, the local "expat community" will be one of your most valuable resources. Most foreign communities can be small, and that which might seem incestuous in time can initially be extremely helpful. You will meet many people who very recently underwent exactly what you are going through now: looking for a job in a strange land. And because of the turnover and transient nature of overseas expat communities, new friends and contacts are eagerly greeted to replace those that have just left.

The people you meet are vital. Meet as many people as you can. Most jobs are filled by word of mouth and the high turnover overseas amongst the expatriate crowd means that your new friends and acquaintances will be your best possible entree to hearing about recently vacated jobs.

If you want to reach out and meet people, there are plenty of places to find and make contacts. Here are some:

Sports: Joining a local sports league can be a great way to meet other foreigners and can be an instant "in" into the foreign community. Most cities around the world have a Hash House Harriers club (a running club) and there should also be rugby teams, softball teams, and sports clubs. Getting involved in sports teams are a good idea on two fronts: In addition to helping you network your way into a job, socializing via sports will also help you keep your sanity and make your adjustment easier.

Social activities: Most cities have "expat associations" built around either a common ethnicity or a common interest. Find a local listing of all the clubs (the local expat community newsletter or web site is a good place to look) and start joining. In addition to formal organizations, there can be a lot of social events: For example, many embassies overseas sponsor a "beer night" and networking socials.

Business resources: Make one of your first stops the American Chamber of Commerce in the city you are in. Sign up for their events and get involved in as many ways as you can. Similarly, you might want to check out Trade Missions.

Advice on International Networking

Vault asked four "international gurus" to share their experiences of networking in a foreign country.

David, China: I already had a job when I arrived in China, but when I was thinking of taking the next step, I got involved with the AmCham Chamber of Commerce in Shanghai. They have a pretty robust organization, with lots of opportunities to get involved in everything from event planning to helping coordinate trade fairs. Through the contacts I met there, I became better integrated into the foreign business scene in Shanghai and was able to make connections that helped me with my job search later.

Michelle, Russia: One of the first events I ever went to after landing in Russia was a meeting of my undergrad alumni association. I would never have gotten involved back home – I always thought you had to be at least 50 to want to do that! – but through the group in Moscow I met a wide range of people, both foreigners and locals, and made some good contacts that helped me with my initial job search. I'm also of German descent, so I decided to also try the German Club of Moscow, but I found it to be a bit stuffy and attended by mostly transferred senior executives and their wives – typical "expatty" stuff. Otherwise, I've met most of my personal and professional acquaintances at expat bars and via initial friends – everyone is very friendly and open to introducing you to others.

Sarah, France: The first thing I did when I landed in Paris was join the American Writers Association in Paris. I wanted to really immerse myself in Parisian culture, but I recognized I would need a lot of support and advice, at least initially while I was getting set up. And it's possible to do it all; I know some people that want to stay away from other Americans while they are in Paris, but I think you can find a balance.

Phil, South Korea: The British Rugby team rocks! You don't have to be British to join, the only requirement is that you be prepared to get dirty and roughed up. Lots of Americans play here, and it's a great sport. Plus, it's at the center of a whole social scene. Every Sunday we play, then meet for beers after. It's a great way to make new friends, improve on existing business contacts, and hear the latest gossip.

Visit Vault at **www.vault.com** for insider company profiles, expert advice, career message boards, expert resume reviews, the Vault Job Board and more.

VAULT CAREER LIBRARY   **137**

Cross-cultural networking

Networking cross-culturally can be, at least initially, somewhat of a challenge. Learn the basic norms of business behavior before you start networking. Familiarize yourself with basics like the importance of business cards, special etiquette rules, and how networking and job hunting is usually done locally. Learn a few courtesy greetings in the local language.

Landing and Getting a Job

Angela followed her boyfriend to India after he was transferred there with a major American bank. She had just graduated from business school, as had her boyfriend, and decided to follow him for both personal and professional reasons. "I had job hunted during school, but only half-heartedly as I knew early on that my boyfriend would be transferred to India. I decided to enjoy business school and worry about finding a job later. I had no idea where to start looking for a job remotely, and many people advised me that I'd be more successful once we actually got to Bombay."

Once in India, Angela started networking. "I found my business school network and all the alumni to be incredibly helpful. I just went through the database (fortunately my school has a very strong alumni database) and sent a cover letter and resume to all the alumni at companies and industries I was interested in. I also found a listing of the best companies to work for in India. I sent my resume and cover letter to the companies listed. The response rate was great, probably much higher than I would have gotten in America. I think people were intrigued by the fact that I was a foreigner looking for work in India, and the MBA degree helped tremendously – it's a great mark of prestige in India, and many of the alumni were in very influential positions."

Frustrations during the job search included trying to get up to date contact information, getting a reliable Internet connection, and not being sure how to navigate companies internally. "A couple of times I was referred by the person I initially contacted to someone else, and because not all the companies had extensive web sites, and because I wasn't really sure how to judge someone's seniority, I was occasionally a little lost about who I was talking to, and why."

With lots of follow up on her initial mailing, Angela started getting interviews and within two months had an offer with a major consumer goods company in marketing. "All in all the process was really painless.

Definitely the MBA and the school helped. I'm not sure I would have been so successful if I didn't have an MBA and some solid previous work experience, but then again my expectations were higher." She finishes: "In the end, I landed a great job, easily comparable to what my classmates are doing back home. In terms of salary, it's probably not as high as if I'd been transferred here from the States, but I'm doing okay. All in all, it was a really interesting experience, and what I like best is how I feel now – like the world is my oyster. I figure if I can land and find a job in India, then hey, I could do the same thing anywhere else in the world!"

Visit Vault at **www.vault.com** for insider company profiles, expert advice,
career message boards, expert resume reviews, the Vault Job Board and more.

V/\ULT CAREER LIBRARY   **139**

Use the Internet's
MOST TARGETED
job search tools.

Vault Job Board

Target your search by industry, function, and experience
level, and find the job openings that you want.

VaultMatch Resume Database

Vault takes match-making to the next level: post your resume
and customize your search by industry, function, experience
and more. We'll match job listings with your interests and
criteria and e-mail them directly to your inbox.

> the most trusted name in career information™

ON THE JOB

What to Expect

No matter how much you've done your homework about the country you're headed to, things will be different once you get there.

Culture Shock

Most of the practical issues of living abroad, such as visas, health insurance and housing have already been covered. Once you arrive in your destination country, however, the single biggest issue will face will be somewhat intangible: culture. Culture is a set of shared, accepted behavior patterns, values, assumptions and common experiences. It defines the social structure, the expectations and the norms of communication for the society.

No matter where you go, you will encounter belief systems different from your own. How intense the differences are, of course, will depend on where you go. If you're heading to England or Australia, the cultural differences, though still there, will not be as marked as the differences you would encounter in, say, Moscow or rural China.

Culture is sometimes mistakenly thought to be just the visible signs of a society, such as the food, the clothes and the houses. With the spread of American movies, literature and cuisine worldwide, it can be tempting to think that cultures are becoming more similar. But it is misleading to think that differences in cultures are eroding: Just because people dress the same and eat the same food, it doesn't mean they think the same. They don't.

For this reason culture is sometimes referred to as an "iceberg" – the visible part (clothes, music, taste in food) being only a very small portion of the whole. The most important aspects of culture (our values, thought processes and belief systems) are hidden below the surface and are not immediately visible.

Visit Vault at **www.vault.com** for insider company profiles, expert advice, career message boards, expert resume reviews, the Vault Job Board and more.

VAULT CAREER LIBRARY   143

The cultural iceberg

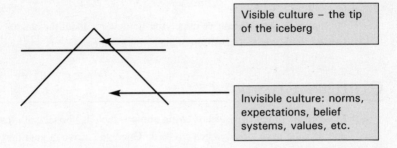

Visible culture – the tip of the iceberg

Invisible culture: norms, expectations, belief systems, values, etc.

When working overseas, it's helpful to keep the iceberg analogy in mind. For example, even if your Swedish office colleagues all wear Western-style suits and speak impeccable English, don't be fooled into assuming they will think and act like you in all situations.

While every culture is different, there are some underlying similarities between groups of cultures. Academicians and anthropologists have attempted to classify the world's cultures into groups bound together by underlying or overarching themes. The most famous of these is probably G. Hofstede's *Cultural Patterns*. Hofstede divided cultures along several lines:

- **Power distance:** How equal/unequal societies are in their distribution of powers

- **Uncertainty avoidance:** The extent to which societies tolerate ambiguity

- **Individualism/collectivism:** How societies value and have allegiance to a group rather than to the individual

- **Achievement/nurturance:** How societies value achievement behaviors vs. nurturing behaviors

While this may seem to be a lot of anthropological lingo, these broad classifications can help you understand and determine how and why the people you come into contact with behave in a certain way. For example, "collectivist" societies place primary importance on the group and the group dynamic. Individual action is not admired. When working in a "collectivist" culture, such as Japan, you might find that individual achievement is not valued as highly as office harmony, and indeed individual actions such as speaking out or having independent thought might not be looked upon as positively as in America (a more "individualistic" society).

While these are very broad generalizations, understanding the types of society may help you predict how co-workers may act in a given situation, and understand their reactions.

Culture shock

So what happens when you come into contact with other cultures and all these overt and hidden differences? You'll experience culture shock. Basically, culture shock is the disorientation you feel in a new environment, and your reaction to that feeling. No matter your situation, and no matter how many times you have traveled before, you should expect to undergo at least some form of culture shock.

Culture shock is a well-documented phenomena (the term was first coined back in 1954). It consists of five distinct stages. You will experience the effects of each stage, though how long each stage will last, and how severe your reaction is, will depend on external variables, such as the environment (how different is it from your home culture?) and your personality (how resilient and adaptive are you?). Interestingly, studies have shown that more self-aware individuals tend to experience more intense culture shock than others, but they also tend to adapt better in the long run.

This graph shows the stages of culture shock, with the initial peak and subsequent decline before returning to equilibrium.

Visit Vault at **www.vault.com** for insider company profiles, expert advice, career message boards, expert resume reviews, the Vault Job Board and more.

V∧ULT CAREER LIBRARY   **145**

The five stages of culture shock are:

1.   **Honeymoon stage:** Your new environment is fantastic. You love everything about it! You embrace it wholeheartedly and experience the world around you with curious eyes. You may even compare your home country unfavorably to your new host country.

2.   **Critical stage:** During this stage you "crash." The euphoria of the first stage disappears. You experience strong feelings of dissatisfaction and become very critical of everything around you. You may experience difficulties in communication and feelings of negativity, impatience, anger and sadness. This is the stage most people think of when they think of "culture shock," and it is also the time when the most damage can be done at work or in social interactions.

3.   **Adjustment stage:** A sense of humor about the situation re-emerges. You realize things aren't all bad. You have a more balanced outlook. You may even feel ashamed of the negative thoughts you previously experienced.

4.   **Adaptation stage:** In this stage you develop a new sense of appreciation for your host culture. You may find yourself adapting some of the customs and habits of the new culture in your daily life. At this point, you've gotten over the worst of culture shock.

5.   **Re-entry stage:** The fifth stage of culture shock refers to the problems of reintegration back to your own country (also called "reverse culture shock").

The important thing to remember about culture shock is that it is entirely natural, and not a personal weakness. But just because it's normal doesn't mean that it's not potentially harmful. Culture shock and the inability to adapt is one of the major reasons for those working abroad to return home.

Vault Tips For Surviving Culture Shock

- **Remember your own culture.** When you're going through a bad phase, surround yourself as much as possible with familiar faces and customs. Don't feel bad about shutting yourself off from the host culture.

- **Don't isolate yourself.** Talk to other expatriates, especially those who've been in country for longer than you have. Chances are very high that most of them have endured culture shock as well. They will be able to help you gain perspective.

- **Recognize that culture shock is natural.** What you are going through is not unique, and you are not the first person who has thought about going home early.

- **Keep fit, both mentally and physically.** Take care of yourself and your general well being. Try to exercise regularly and eat healthy foods.

- **Above all, keep your sense of humor.**

Visit Vault at **www.vault.com** for insider company profiles, expert advice, career message boards, expert resume reviews, the Vault Job Board and more.

VAULT CAREER LIBRARY   147

Work Environment

A key challenge when landing in a new environment is adapting to the new work environment and professional culture. When you start a new job abroad, your challenge is twofold: Not only do you have to adapt to a new office culture, but that office culture will be heavily influenced by the external culture of the society, with which you are also unfamiliar. It's a double whammy, and navigating a new professional environment in an unfamiliar country can be a minefield.

Regardless of your destination, there will be differences in your new work environment from what you are accustomed to back home. There will be different professional norms and expectations, and different ways of interacting with your co-workers.

This is true even if you are being transferred overseas with a company you have worked for previously. Just because you're working for a company with the same name and the same logo, don't expect your new workplace to resemble your home office! If you go in with that expectation, it will be easier to adjust your attitude upwards than come in for a rude awakening.

Before you go, make sure you have thoroughly researched the culture of your destination country. Buy a good guidebook. The Culture Shock! series of books, published by Graphic Arts Center and currently covering 72 countries, are a good source of information on business culture, etiquette, and professional norms for your destination. Try to master the basics before you go: how to greet people, how to exchange business cards, etc.

But, don't expect to master everything from books or self-study. No amount of "study" before you go will prevent you from making mistakes. But that's fine – you're expected to make mistakes! Also, remember that to your host country, you are an American, and they will expect you to act as an American. They will not expect the same standard of behavior from you, though they will be pleased if you adopt their habits, especially in gestures of politeness and business etiquette.

The following list points to some of the major areas where you might expect to encounter significant differences in the work environment.

- **Work hours and level of activity at work.** Some cultures are more focused on "face time" than others: You might have to be prepared to spend considerable time in the office after official work hours are over, even if you have nothing to do. For example, in some cultures, it is inappropriate for junior employees to leave before the boss does. Likewise, you might find your co-workers more intense, or perhaps more laid-back, than at home.

- **Formality and bureaucracy within the office.** American work environments tend to be rather informal, and the boss/subordinate relationship can sometimes be very friendly. This is quite unique, and unless your destination is Canada or Australia, you will probably encounter more formality in the office environment than you are used to. Don't expect to become best buddies with your boss.

- **Socializing with co-workers.** This is another area where you might encounter differences. Depending on the situation, you might be expected to socialize frequently with your co-workers outside of office hours. Again, it all depends on the culture. In parts of Europe, for example, you may be asked to visit your co-workers homes frequently. In Asia, by contrast, you may go drinking with your colleagues, but you usually won't be invited back to their houses.

- **Resistance or respect.** The way you are treated by co-workers, either subtly or not so subtly, can differ. There may be resistance to your arrival from local employees who may resent you for any number of reasons. They may suspect you are paid more than they are, or the previous foreigner working at the company made a bad impression, or who knows? Be prepared for negative stereotypes.

But on the positive side, you may be treated with more respect than you would be accorded back home. The feeling of being special and unique can give you quite a buzz, but don't confuse politeness with reality. The international language of hard work still applies!

- **Level of responsibility.** Finally, if you've been transferred by your company, be prepared for a change in the level of responsibility. Corresponding titles and seemingly similar job descriptions might mean very different things in different offices. Depending on the situation, you might have to be prepared to prove yourself all over again.

Visit Vault at **www.vault.com** for insider company profiles, expert advice,
career message boards, expert resume reviews, the Vault Job Board and more.

VAULT CAREER LIBRARY   **149**

Fitting In At Your New Workplace

- If your company has transferred you, make an effort to keep in touch with what's going on back home. Engage mentors from your home office and communicate with them regularly. Network and outreach to other offices in the region, and build a professional support network around you.

- Learn the social boundaries, professional norms and business etiquette of your new office. Be as observant as possible. Learn how things are done in your new environment and adapt.

- Reach out to the local employees and be as friendly and approachable (within the confines of the culture) as appropriate. Again, learn the basics of business etiquette and social interactions. Though you may be initially inclined to socialize with the other foreigners in the office, you can learn as much or more, both about the country and the business, from the locals.

Guide to Business Etiquette

Here is a look at different business customs in various parts of the world:

Working in Japan? Give business cards with two hands, and spend a lot of time admiring and examining the card. The more time you spend indicates the more respect you have for the person.

Working in Korea? Only give things with your right hand, never with your left. And never, ever, leave work before your supervisors.

Working in France? Don't expect to be on a first name basis with your boss, even if you've been working in France for years.

Working in Colombia? Look sideways – direct eye contact is seen as overly aggressive, not as a sign of forthrightness.

Working in Argentina? Think you're doing business with 'just' a company? Think again! You're actually developing personal relationships with a whole slew of people…. The same applies for most of Latin America and the Middle East.

Working in Taiwan? Never write anyone's name in red ink – red is the color of death and writing a personal name in red is akin to a death threat.

Working in Russia? Don't be surprised if you're greeted by a hug and a kiss.

Working in Germany? Expect to call close business partners by their formal surnames, even years after you first meet them. No "Hi Bob!" for you.

Working in India? Don't be surprised if your Indian colleague says 'Yes' while shaking his head. He still means yes.

Working in China? Don't sit opposite the door during a business dinner – or you will be expected to pick up the entire tab.

Working in Brazil? Avoid giving gifts that contain the color purple – it's associated with death.

Working in the Middle East? Don't think about scheduling anything for Friday – it's the equivalent of the American Saturday.

Visit Vault at **www.vault.com** for insider company profiles, expert advice, career message boards, expert resume reviews, the Vault Job Board and more.

V/\ULT CAREER LIBRARY 151

Social Life

Your personal life may come under scrutiny away from home. The line between professional and social lives can blur overseas. Be especially careful about your behavior outside of the office. Expats tend to stand out more. Often expat communities are very small and sometimes claustrophobic. Rumors and gossip may travel fast. Above all, be discreet.

Much depends on how many other fellow expatriates you know, and how much you choose to immerse yourself in the "expat" scene or "go local." This doesn't have to be a black and white choice; you will probably find yourself at different times switching between various groups as your comfort with, and interest in, the local culture waxes and wanes.

Generally speaking, if you're in a smaller town or in a situation where there are few foreigners, the local people will be friendlier. Take advantage of their hospitality and take the opportunity to really immerse yourself in the culture, an opportunity you may not get in a larger city where you'll naturally be drawn more to people like yourself.

In-Country Resources

Government and legal resources

As already mentioned, register with your embassy once you arrive, and check out what resources they have for resident foreigners. This will vary greatly on the size and scope of each individual embassy. Check out the travel section of the United States State Department web site – www.state.gov/travel/ – it will help you understand what you can expect of the local embassy.

Living resources

There are a variety of Internet sites devoted to the overseas living experience. Here, you can connect with other people in similar situations, or browse others' experiences of their time abroad. These sites also have helpful links to practical and travel-related matters.

Some top sites include:

- www.expatforum.com – Resources and a chat forum organized by country

- www.monster.com – Has chat boards and articles for people working abroad

- www.lp.com – The Lonely Planet web site has evolved into a vibrant virtual community

- www.transitionsabroad.com – Publishes a (subscriber fee) bimonthly magazine for those working and studying abroad, but also has a host of information on the free access site

Visit Vault at **www.vault.com** for insider company profiles, expert advice, career message boards, expert resume reviews, the Vault Job Board and more.

VAULT CAREER LIBRARY   153

Day in the Life Abroad

CHAPTER 9

What's it really like working in another country?   Follow these five international workers through a typical day in their lives as they work abroad.

ESL Teacher, South Korea

Mark is a teacher of English as a Second Language (ESL) in Seoul, South Korea.

6:00 a.m.: Get up and jump in the shower. It's early, too early, but you've got to get to downtown Seoul and beat through the early morning traffic. Your first class is at 7:00 a.m. You catch the bus right outside your door and hop on for a ride through the dark streets of Seoul. Even though it's early, the bus is crowded.

6:50 a.m.: Arrive at the Institute and get a cup of hot instant coffee. The newer teachers are already there, anxiously preparing their lesson plans for the morning, just like you when you first arrived. You've been doing this for six months now, and you know most of your lesson plans by heart. Goodbye, preparation time!

7:00 a.m.: Greet your first class, a group of eager professionals. They are anxious to get in their hour of English before they start their jobs at various banks and corporations. It's an advanced class, and most of the students have been at the Institute for several semesters. It's a relaxed and friendly class, despite the early hour. The topic for today? It's a "free talking" class; one of the students has selected the topic of military conscription.

10:00 a.m.: Time for a short break. You've already taught three 50-minute classes. You hang out with the other teachers in the teacher's lounge, and grab a quick game of cards with a couple of British teachers. With 10 minutes before your next class, you stop playing to prepare a bit; it's heavy on grammar, and you need to do some technical research.

11:30 a.m.: Say goodbye to your last class for the morning, a group of students studying for their university entrance exams. You've just spent an hour with them discussing the difference between "had" and "has had." Luckily, most of the teaching at this Institute is not as dry.

12:00 p.m.: Grab a quick lunch with an Australian co-worker at the little restaurant round the corner. You've become addicted to the food in Korea, and slurp your cold chili noodles happily. And at only $1.50 a bowl, it's the best deal in town.

1:00 p.m.: Time to catch a bus across town to your first private tutoring lesson. This is where the real money is, and although your "split shift" at the Institute is a real pain (you have morning classes, and late evening classes, but nothing in between) it leaves your afternoons free for private lessons, where you can earn three times your Institute salary per hour.

2:00 p.m.: You're having a conversation about cosmetics with a group of housewives. You don't think they learn too much (this class is only an hour a week) and you guess it's more about socializing than the English for them. For you too. You've made some good friends in this class – one of the women has invited you out to visit her husband's mushroom farm in the country this weekend.

3:30 p.m.: Your last private lesson of the day is over. You've got a few hours to kill before your next class at the Institute at 7 p.m. Too short a time to go home, too long to do anything else. You stop in at an Internet cafe to catch up on the latest news from home, then you hang out in the park for a while, creating a game for a group of kindergarten students you will teach tomorrow.

9:00 p.m.: The long teaching day is over! You head out with a group of foreign teachers to a nearby bar. You relax and have a few beers. There are a couple of Canadians, two Brits and a Swede with impeccable English. Some are new, though most have been in the country for a while. Meeting all the different teachers, as well as the students, is one of the best perks of the job. In the noisy bar, tables of Korean businessmen are drinking and celebrating. If it were Friday, you'd probably continue drinking and then go on to a nightclub or a Korean karaoke bar. But it's Wednesday, and everyone has an early start tomorrow. You take a cab home – it's almost as cheap as the bus.

Marketing Associate, Uruguay

Andrea is a marketing associate working for a company in Montevideo, Uruguay.

7:00 a.m.: You've just finished dressing for work when Clara, your cleaning lady, walks in. Your company-provided apartment, while not that big, is nonetheless pleasantly situated and comes with cleaning service included. Greet her and finish your coffee, and get ready to leave.

7:10 a.m.: The office is only a 10-minute walk away from your apartment. You'll be just in time for the early morning meeting with the finance department. The day starts earlier here, but luckily it finishes earlier too.

9:00 a.m.: Two meetings later and it's only 9 a.m.! And you've got a busy morning ahead of you. As well as Uruguay, a small but relatively affluent country in South America, your office covers territory in Paraguay and Bolivia – adjoining countries that don't have large enough markets to support their own offices. This afternoon you have a conference call scheduled with the category manager for all of Southern South America. She's based in Argentina, and wants to know your budget figures for a proposed line extension for all three countries.

11:10 a.m.: A few calls come in from headquarters in the States. Luckily there's no time difference between Uruguay and Minnesota, so communication is easy – but becomes all too frequent! You talk to the media, budgeting and product development people about the latest figures you sent off for a badly performing product here in your three countries. Though you never worked for this company in the United States, you get the impression that you're doing a whole lot more down here by yourself – in a smaller office, a lot more falls onto your plate. It's frustrating, too – you often feel as though your colleagues and managers in the U.S. don't really understand what's going on down here.

12:00 p.m.: You grab a quick lunch in the office cafeteria with two Uruguayan colleagues.

1:30 p.m.: You direct all calls through to your answering machine and hunker down with the spreadsheet. The big conference call is at 4 p.m.

2:00 p.m.: Right in the middle of a spreadsheet analysis, with the presentation to create for tomorrow, the office computer system crashes yet again. You try to relax – there's nothing you can do. It's all in the hands of the technicians now. You talk with a colleague and listen as she talks about her weekend at the beach. You're tired after the hectic morning, and reflect ruefully that Uruguay is one of the only Latin American countries that doesn't have a siesta. One would be good right now – if you didn't have the conference call coming up, of course.

3:35 p.m.: The computers are back up, and the numbers are looking good. Though the three countries are similar in size, their economies and

Visit Vault at **www.vault.com** for insider company profiles, expert advice, career message boards, expert resume reviews, the Vault Job Board and more.

VAULT CAREER LIBRARY   **157**

demographics are vastly different. You reflect, not for the first time, that you're probably doing the job of three people.

3:45 p.m.: Your assistant and travel coordinator comes in to talk about your trip to Paraguay and Bolivia next week. You'll be meeting with merchandisers, sales reps and some local advertising agencies there. You ask her to come back after the call – you need to clear your head.

4:30 p.m.: The call went well, and the category manager liked your numbers. There's still a lot of work to be done, and all-important decisions to come from the States, but it looks like the line extension will be launched in your territory over the next three months. You take a quick tea break, then start making phone calls for your trip next week.

6:00 p.m.: You finish up for the day and catch a cab to the French Embassy. It's Bastille Day, July 14th, and the French Embassy is holding a garden party to celebrate. Free wine and cheese! You know some expats from the French community – in a small city like Montevideo, all the foreigners tend to know each other.

7:15 p.m.: The French national anthem has been sung, and the reception is in full swing. After a full day working in Spanish, you're happy to chat in English with some American friends. You drink wine and talk, all the time thinking about your telephone call and the decisions this afternoon: Is it too early to enter the Bolivian market?

Importer, Mexico

With her partner based in Chicago, Mary imports ceramic garden art from Mexico and sells it in a store back home.

6:00 a.m.: Up early. I only make these buying trips four times a year, so it's essential to make the most of every minute. Today, I've got two visits to make, and I want to be back at the motel before dark.

6:30 a.m.: I join Sandra in the motel's breakfast room. Sandra is a student at the University of Mexico. I found after posting an ad on the university's bulletin board, and she's been helping us out on these trips ever since. I speak good enough Spanish, but certainly not enough to negotiate in.

7:00 a.m.: We go out to the truck – luckily, it's still there. My biggest fear about these trips is the truck. Stealing cars is a bit of a hobby in this part of Mexico, and I consider myself lucky that so far there have been no problems.

I check the back. All the products we have bought are still there. Good. And there's enough room for another few boxes. We climb in and set off.

7:35 a.m.: Sandra's driving; we'll take turns throughout the day. Today is our last day visiting suppliers and buying for the next quarter. My mind is whirring, going through all the details I'll need to take care of for the trip back across the border in two days. My biggest learning about being an entrepreneur so far? You've got to take care of everything – there are no "departments" in a start-up!

9:00 a.m.: We reach our first village, one we've never visited or dealt with before. Sandra got us this contact. She keeps her eyes open all year round and occasionally visits trade shows for us in Mexico City. We meet the potential supplier, a smiling guy in his 50s who shows off his workroom proudly.

9:30 a.m.: Unfortunately, I don't like the stuff. It looks good from afar, but up close I can see faint cracking in many of the pieces, especially the larger urns and statues. Not a good sign. After a year of doing this, I know that my biggest problem is the poor quality of some of the goods. As we buy upfront, we have to be really careful.

10:00 a.m.: I buy a piece from them for personal use, but decline to enter into any kind of bulk agreement. We leave with promises of returning next year to see if they've made any improvements.

10:15 a.m.: On the road again. We could do our buying an easier way, via distributors in Mexico City or Tijuana, but truth be told, I enjoy visiting the actual artists and their workrooms. Even with running the truck, travel costs and Sandra's salary, it still works out cheaper in the long run. And by buying directly I can pay the artists slightly more than a big distributor would. The travel is tiring but exciting: Mexico is just beautiful outside of the smog of the big cities. But dangerous – a huge truck appears out of nowhere and overtakes us on the narrow mountain road.

12:00 p.m.: We arrive at Los Sacos, the village of one of our oldest and favorite suppliers. The whole family comes out to greet us. They work together in the small factory behind the house, and seeing them all is like coming back to old friends.

12:33 p.m.: Chicken soup and fried enchiladas for lunch – yum!

1:30 p.m.: I'm going over the merchandise – it's good, really good. I agree to buy enough to fill six boxes – more than I anticipated, but since I didn't buy anything in the last village there's enough room in the truck. We haggle

Visit Vault at www.vault.com for insider company profiles, expert advice, career message boards, expert resume reviews, the Vault Job Board and more.

VAULT CAREER LIBRARY **159**

a little over prices, but still keep it friendly. I'm a little worried, though – he's pushing the prices higher on me, cutting into my markup.

3:30 p.m.: Everything's finally packed up and we drive away. It's my turn to drive, and while I concentrate on the road I think about Juan and his prices.

4:00 p.m.: I'm still worried about it. Maybe we could pay the higher prices if he'd bring his stuff to us, say in Mexico City. But then I'd miss seeing the factory, and his new designs. That's the downside of working remotely, or via distributors – remoteness and lack of trust, and the weakening of our strong relationship.

5:15 p.m.: We arrive back at the motel without any breakdowns! I thank Sandra and say goodbye. We talked in the car a little bit about her taking more of an active role. She's graduating soon and won't be as free to come on these trips unless we offer her something more permanent. I'd hate to lose her, but I'm not sure if we're big enough to warrant taking on a "real" employee. If we expanded to that store that wanted to carry our stuff in Cleveland...

6:00 p.m.: Time for a quick dip in the pool to get rid of the dust.

6:00 p.m.: I call Tracy, my partner back in Chicago. We discuss my concerns about Juan. She updates me on what's been going on in the store – a large order came through from a housing complex that's starting near us. Excellent news! I say my goodbyes and promise to see her in four days.

7:00 p.m.: More enchiladas, this time under the stars. I enjoy the time by myself and the soft breeze. I sip my daiquiri. All in all, a successful trip, but as usual it's raised a lot of questions. I think about the shop – business is starting to take off as we get established. If we grow it or expand to other locations, trips like these won't be feasible – I couldn't take the time off. We'd need more support on the ground – maybe Sandra, and she knows the business. Or we'll have to consider distributors, instead of going directly to the villages.

9:00 p.m.: I turn in early. I've got a long day ahead of me tomorrow, preparing all the paperwork for the border crossing. And I'm absolutely exhausted, both physically and mentally. Another thing I never realized about being an entrepreneur – how difficult it is to turn your brain off!

Peace Corps Volunteer, Senegal

Mark is a Peace Corps Volunteer in Senegal, West Africa.

6:30 a.m.: Thwunk! Thwunk! The sound has been creeping into my sleep for about an hour now, and I finally wake up and acknowledge it. Outside my hut, the women of the village have been up pounding millet.

7:15 a.m.: I dress without showering. With no electricity or running water, a shower in the morning is a luxury. Plus, I know I'm going to get dirty today, so what's the point?

7:45 a.m.: Time for a leisurely breakfast in the family compound. We all sleep in our own huts, and meet in the middle for meals and socializing. I sit on a raised dais and drink the local coffee – bitter but good. As I drink, I think about what I have to do today: the upcoming meeting, the state of my motorcycle – do I have enough gas?

8:00 a.m.: I wave goodbye to my host family – the men are heading out to the fields and the women are cooking or going out on water runs. I hop on my motorcycle – with 50 villages in my area of responsibility, good, reliable transport is a major concern. Luckily this little guy hasn't let me down yet.

8:30 a.m.: I drive along the dusty roads and wave to the occasional villager I see. After two years here, they all know me, and I know most of them.

9:15 a.m.: I arrive at my target village, dusty and hot. Even though it's still relatively early, the sun seems impossibly high in the sky, like it's been every day. Senegal is one of the hottest places on earth. Sometimes, I feel like I spend every day just sweating.

9:30 a.m.: The women of the village are slowly gathering in one of the central compounds around me. Today is our fifth meeting, and we're actually going to get started on the project we've been talking about for two months now: planting a fruit orchard. The women will use the fruit to supplement their family's diets, or to sell for some surplus cash at the market.

10:00 a.m.: All the women have finally arrived. Time is a different concept here: Having everyone together an hour after the meeting was scheduled is actually great. Heck, I was even 10 minutes late! I explain what we're going to be doing today, and then we all head down to the field that's designated to be the orchard.

10:45 a.m.: We're hard at work in the future orchard, carefully preparing the fruit seedlings in little bags of soil and lining them up in the ground. As we

Visit Vault at **www.vault.com** for insider company profiles, expert advice, career message boards, expert resume reviews, the Vault Job Board and more.

VAULT CAREER LIBRARY   **161**

work, the women chatter and tease me. They all want to know when I'm going to bring my girlfriend to live in the compound. The fact that I don't have a girlfriend doesn't seem to stop them! They also ask about my family, and tell me about theirs.

12:00 p.m.: A good morning's work, and time to get out of the sun. I have lunch at one of the compounds and share news with the men of my host family. Then a short nap, a quick play with some of the smaller kids, and then it's time to be off. I'll be back next month when the seedlings start to sprout.

1:30 p.m.: I head toward the nearest town, realizing I've actually got a free afternoon. This is a rarity – with the number of villages I'm responsible for, I usually have two or even three meetings in a given day. This is good – I've got some shopping to do, not to mention getting some more gas for the motorcycle...

2:30 p.m.: Fuda is the central town around here, a hub for all the villages in the area. I wander through the market, picking out some vegetables for my family. They don't receive a stipend for hosting me, so I try to help out in other ways. Buying some vegetables to add to the family's cooking budget (and I've got to admit – vary my diet!) is a good way to help out.

3:30 p.m.: I buy potatoes, tomatoes, onions, a couple of delicious-looking oranges, gas for my motorcycle and a new shirt for myself. I've still got time and energy, so I stop by a local bar. I hope to see one or both of the other Peace Corps volunteers that serve in the area, but I'm out of luck.

4:00 p.m.: I down a local beer – like the coffee it's bitter but good! I chat with the owners of the bar and a couple of men who have sought refuge on the cool patio. They all know me by now, and after studying the local language fairly intensively during my first year I'm now comfortable enough to talk about anything.

4:30 p.m.: No more beer, I have a long drive ahead of me back to my village. I leave a note for the other volunteers, telling them I'll be back on Saturday, and to look for me. Then it's back on the motorcycle and the dusty roads.

6:00 p.m.: My favorite time of the day. The work is over, I've had my shower, and the heat is subsiding as the sun starts to set. All around the village, people are drifting between compounds, talking and catching up on the news of the day. We have plenty of visitors over at our house. I relax on our dais in the middle of the compound, trying to forget about the busy day I have ahead of me tomorrow.

8:00 p.m.: Supper is prepared by my eight-year-old "niece," who is just learning to cook. Tonight it's chicken and a rice mixture we eat with our hands. The sun is setting now, and after eating we lie back on the dais, staring up at the sky. We talk about astronomy and the stars, then listen to the BBC on the radio for a while. Afterward, we discuss international politics and the state of the world. The villagers are very interested in the world outside, and since I've come to live here I've become much more aware of world events too. Funny to think that in a tiny village on the edge of Africa the people are more informed than in some of the biggest cities back home.

10:00 p.m.: My host dad wakes me gently. I've drifted off to sleep outside on the dais, and now it's time to go to my hut and my real bed.

MBA Consultant in Uzbekistan

MBA Enterprise, the Peace Corps for the MBA-crowd, places recent MBA grads in positions to act as management and business consultants under a USAID program. Placements are heavily focused in central Asia and Eastern Europe. It's a small program, and very competitive – in 2003, only 10 positions were available for 98 applicants. Prior experience working abroad is a definite asset. Check out www.mbaec-cdc.org for more information on postings, qualifications, and how to apply. Here's a look at a day in the life of Shaun, an MBA in Uzbekistan.

6:00 a.m.: The alarm goes off. I groan and roll over. I have to get up this early in order to squeeze in an hour of Russian lessons before work. It's only a quick walk to the office. I'm in Ferghana, a regional capital in Uzbekistan. In this town, nothing is very far.

7:30 a.m.: I'm in the middle of my Russian lesson with Oksana. Even though Uzbekistan isn't officially part of Russia anymore, Russian is definitely the lingua franca of the region. Everyone speaks it, especially for business. I'm already somewhat fluent – I took Russian lessons before I arrived, but I've still got miles to go. To put it mildly, Russian is a tough language to learn – very difficult and very frustrating! Of course, I get a lot of practice – outside of the office, there aren't too many English speakers.

8:30 a.m.: The lesson is over and the rest of the staff are starting to trickle in. There's 15 of us, and we're set up by USAID to provide business training, advice and trade promotion to companies in the region. I'm in charge, overseeing all the functions of the office. It's a very hands-on role – lots of management responsibility! The rest of the staff are bright, young Uzbekis, all of whom, thank goodness, speak English. Two have studied in the States,

Visit Vault at **www.vault.com** for insider company profiles, expert advice, career message boards, expert resume reviews, the Vault Job Board and more.

VAULT CAREER LIBRARY   **163**

and a couple have MBAs. They act as business advisors to the companies in the region.

9:15 a.m.: My first order of business is to meet with one of the staff, Doniyor. He has just returned from vacation and I need to get him up to speed. We have a new EVA (experienced volunteer advisor) arriving today. EVAs are retired, experienced professionals from the States who are contracted by USAID to come and lend their expertise to local companies. The one who's arriving this afternoon is an expert in agribusiness and export, and he'll be working with three local companies to improve their marketing plans.

10:00 a.m.: Together we finalize the plan. The general goal of an EVA is to provide one or two improvements in each company – we call these "successes." Successes are things like increased sales, better margins, increased employment, more exports, etc. The goal for this EVA and his three client companies? Increased sales and exports.

10:10 a.m.: Doniyor is ready to go and meet him at the airport.

11:00 a.m.: Another meeting, this time with an EVA who is leaving soon. We review the outcome of his work with two local producers of sun-dried tomatoes. Jim is a fantastic guy with loads of experience – more than 25 years. He's had a wonderful impact with the companies, setting them up with new export markets and increased sales. For me, it's doubly useful: I learn a tremendous amount from the companies we work with, and also from the EVAs. It's a powerful mixture.

12:20 p.m.: I'm helping one of the staff rework a report. For each "success" in the region, we write a report called a "success story." These are then submitted to the USAID office to show the results of the program. The "successes" are tangible demonstrations of our impact on the company, and on the economy of the region. There is an emphasis on real results here – something that pleasantly surprised me when I first arrived, and something I hadn't normally associated with development work.

1:00 p.m.: Lunch at my desk – again! The office generally closes early, around 5 or 6 p.m., but the hours in between are jam-packed. I don't want to miss a call that's coming in from Afghanistan. They're requesting a transfer of one of our business advisors to help out with a new regional office they're setting up.

2:00 p.m.: I'm on the phone to Moscow and the United States, trying to secure a quality management EVA who can work with local companies to improve internal operations. But getting the EVA is only half the battle: On the other hand, we also need to find qualified local companies who are willing to participate in the program. Though most of the companies around here can benefit from the help, a lot of them aren't too keen on the idea of a foreigner coming in and possibly peering through all their books.

3:00 p.m.: The new EVA has arrived from the airport. I introduce him around the office, and have a brief chat. We'll talk more in depth tomorrow, but right now he's tired and needs to get to his hotel.

5:00 p.m.: Early finish today – it's soccer time! Every Tuesday we have a weekly soccer match against a local group of kids. The game is practically mandatory for the whole office.

7:00 p.m.: I'm exhausted – two hours of soccer is more than enough for me. We head as a group to a local bar for some "plov" (a meat and rice pilaf) and vodka – the Uzbek equivalent of pizza and beer. I could talk and drink all night with my colleagues, but I suspect I'll turn in early – Russian lessons again tomorrow morning!

Returning Home

CHAPTER 10

Practicalities

Your time abroad is coming to an end. While you may be sad to leave, you recognize, for any number of reasons, that it's time to move on. Your contract is over, or you've got grad school plans, or you just simply want to go home.

You have much to consider as you leave your host country. In addition to all the usual moving-related issues you'll have to deal with, take into consideration these issues too:

- Make sure you understand what you are owed upon completion of your contract – returned damage deposits, airfare home, etc.

- Acquaint yourself with the exit criteria for your host country. In many countries there are strict limits on what you can bring out of the country in terms of cash or money. If this is the case, make sure you've figured out how you'll get your savings transferred.

- Understand your legal status in the country once your contract comes to an end. Your last day of work will probably not be your last day in the country. To avoid a nasty surprise at the airport on your way out, make sure you're covered (legally) until the day you leave, including for any vacation time you may want to take in the country.

- At work, make sure you've got hard copies of references. If you've been studying, make sure you've got all your diplomas or certifications (including certified copies), and know where and how to get additional copies.

- If necessary, network. Before you leave your host country, lay the groundwork for networking possibilities back home. Cast your net wide and reach out to friends, acquaintances, co-workers and students who might know people back home you should contact.

- Finally, don't forget to plan a goodbye party for yourself! Make sure all of your new contacts and friends have your contact information.

To help ease the transition, there are several steps to follow. First, and probably most importantly, take time to decompress and deal with your re-entry shock. Don't leap into a job hunt. Says Todd, after coming out of a two-year stint in the Peace Corps: "For the first three months back, I just traveled around the States, meeting old friends, renewing acquaintances, and

Visit Vault at www.vault.com for insider company profiles, expert advice, career message boards, expert resume reviews, the Vault Job Board and more.

VAULT CAREER LIBRARY   167

just enjoying exploring my country. Having no expectations of myself really helped during what could have been a very stressful time, and it was also interesting – I showed myself that the United States could be just as interesting as living in another culture."

Reverse Culture Shock

The experience of returning home and the associated problems is the fifth stage of culture shock, referred to as "re-entry shock" or "reverse culture shock." Some experts in the field consider reverse culture shock to be even more traumatic than simple culture shock. While we expect living internationally to be tough, most don't realize that returning home can be equally difficult.

Experiencing reverse culture shock is a natural part of the transition process for everyone coming home. How severely you experience it depends on a whole host of factors, such as the length of time you were away, where you were and the type of person you are. Once you return home, you might experience some of these symptoms of reverse culture shock:

- Difficulty in relating to others. After your time abroad, you may have experienced significant personal growth compared to the friends and family you "left behind." You have changed, and the way you see the world and perceive things has also changed. Because of this, you may have difficulty relating to friends you were once close to. You may even feel like a foreigner in your own country.

- Boredom and lack of stimulation. Coming home may seem dull. You may miss the excitement of your time outside the country.

- Feelings of criticism and disapproval. You may find yourself critical of things back home in a way you weren't before you left. You will probably also experience homesickness for the place you have just left, and find yourself comparing your home culture unfavorably to your previous residence.

- Professional boredom. If you're going back to work for the same company that transferred you overseas in the first place, you might find yourself stifled. It's possible you were used to greater freedom and often less bureaucracy abroad, and the amount of independence and responsibility you experienced abroad may be cut once you return home. This is a common complaint among employees being transferred back to their home offices after time abroad. The more senior the employee, the more serious the situation. It has been estimated that two thirds of all corporate transfers leave the company within two years of "coming home."

Re-entry shock will eventually pass. The length of time before you are truly comfortable again in your home setting will vary from weeks to even years. Some people who have spent significant time in another culture and adapted very heavily into their "new" culture may never fully feel at home again.

The following are a series of hints to make the transition easier and lessen the effects of re-entry shock:

• Remember what you're feeling is perfectly normal.

• Don't beat yourself up if you have changed and your friends and family haven't. Explore new places and attempt to connect with new people. Find a community of people that have spent time abroad or who have a more international outlook, and surround yourself with like-minded people. You'll still have your old friends, but you'll also have new friends.

• Keep in touch with friends and contacts from your host country, and treat yourself to things that remind you of and keep you in touch with your time abroad.

• Don't over-romanticize your time spent outside the country. You came back for a reason.

Leveraging Your International Experience

Your time abroad may have enabled you to develop valuable skills. Just about any aspect of business, including marketing, HR and finance, can profit from your international experience.

Highlight your international experience

You've gained more from your international experience than you realize. Aside from your specific work responsibilities or course of study, you've also learned to face challenges and cope with situations outside the norm.

You may have developed skills in areas like project management, consensus building, creativity and coping with primitive living conditions – not to mention any language skills you've acquired. Now you must translate this experience, tangible and not, in a way employers will understand.

Visit Vault at **www.vault.com** for insider company profiles, expert advice,
career message boards, expert resume reviews, the Vault Job Board and more.

VAULT CAREER LIBRARY   **169**

Make a "reverse international inventory." List your experiences – professional skills and accomplishments as well as volunteer and club involvement. Think about the skills you developed. What character traits did you develop? What challenges did you overcome?

Once you have listed all your activities and accomplishments abroad, you may want to hone in on three or four areas that you really felt you developed while overseas. Back up each new skill or area of improvement with concrete examples.

Networking

One of the advantages you have when returning home from a period abroad is the existence of an additional network group. If you've gone abroad with an organization or a sponsoring outfit, your network will include all prior participants in the program. For example, the Peace Corps has a very strong and active alumni association to help with job searching and re-entry transition.

Even if you go through a formal organization, you still have a strong, albeit more informal, network. For example, you can now consider everyone who has worked in the same city or country part of your network. People are always willing to help the familiar, and this can be in your favor.

International experience is also a great way to establish a common bond during an interview with a recruiter or a potential employer. Just as by virtue of being overseas you have something in common with every foreigner you meet (you're all foreigners), returning home can engender the same type of emotional connection. You might find in talking to potential employer that they too have worked abroad.

Translating your international experience

One of the key challenges you will face upon returning home is how to adequately capture your international experience and translate it effectively for potential employers. While international experience can be a great resume booster, it can also be problematic. A traditional recruiter for a traditional company may have difficulty relating to your time away. They may not understand your motivations, or may not be familiar with the company, even the job description. It may be difficult for potential employers to place you into the right context and understand what you did and what skills you learned.

Michelle, who worked in Russia and China for six years, describes feeling like an "exotic creature" in front of potential employers. "They would ooh and aah about my interesting background. I found I was able to very easily get interviews, but when it came to actually getting a job, I felt recruiters would go with a 'safer bet.'"

Sarah, who worked in Shanghai at a small consulting company, found that translating her experiences into language recruiters could understand was a challenge. "My experiences in China certainly helped me get into business school, but I discovered when I was applying for jobs that many of the recruiters were looking for applicants from traditional backgrounds that they could understand, or who had "proven themselves" at a Goldman or a Kraft. The number of times the recruiter's eyes glazed over when I tried to explain what I had been doing! Often, I felt they just didn't get it."

One way to overcome this problem is to be as explicit as possible on your resume. For example, let's say you worked at a small financial services company in London. A recruiter or potential employer will want to know: How big was the company? What was its niche or specialty? What exactly were you doing?

Or let's say you worked with a media company in Bangkok. You need to be able to convey the type of company it was (size, history, reputation, position in the marketplace), what your position was and how you related to others in the office, etc. Of course, it's not feasible to include all this detail on your resume, but be prepared to explain or offer this auxiliary information in the interests of clarity and context during an interview. On your resume, you should consider adding a "tag line" that places your company in context. For example:

"The largest HR Consulting company in Mainland China"
"Fastest growing media company in Italy"

Now you're ready to take on the world. Good luck!

Visit Vault at **www.vault.com** for insider company profiles, expert advice, career message boards, expert resume reviews, the Vault Job Board and more.

VAULT CAREER LIBRARY   **171**

Use the Internet's
MOST TARGETED
job search tools.

Vault Job Board

Target your search by industry, function, and experience
level, and find the job openings that you want.

VaultMatch Resume Database

Vault takes match-making to the next level: post your resume
and customize your search by industry, function, experience
and more. We'll match job listings with your interests and
criteria and e-mail them directly to your inbox.

APPENDIX

Appendix

General Country Research

Center for World Indigenous Studies - www.cwis.rg
Focuses on the "Fourth World." A good source of papers and facts.

CIA Factbook - www.cia.gov
Very academic. Very detailed treasure trove of factual information about every country in the world.

Country Profiles - www.about.com
Basic facts and research about most countries, as well as articles and links to other resources.

The Economist - www.economist.com
60 Country Profiles, in-depth snapshots with additional articles, resources, links and statistics

Lonely Planet - www.lp.com
Travelers' tales make good, informal and informative reading if you're thinking about living, as well as traveling, in a given country. Huge web site and virtual community, with interesting and informative posts from travelers on almost every region of the world.

One World - www.oneworld.net.
Great resource for anyone interested in development and emerging economies. Jobs, volunteer opportunities, country specific information news updates and more.

U.S. Commercial Service - www.buyusa.gov
Has a section entitled "Doing Business," which offers profiles of every major country with special emphasis on their business climate and economy.

Volunteering Databases and Directories

Action Without Borders - www.idealist.org
Possibly the largest comprehensive database on the web focused on development and non-profit work. Thousands of organizations are listed here, and a helpful search engine allows you to search by internship or volunteer opportunities.

Association of Voluntary Service Organizations - www.avso.org

A European-based non-profit. Extensive links to volunteer programs.

Catholic Network of Volunteer Services - www.cnvs.org
Directory of Catholic and other Christian volunteer organizations.

Center for International Education Exchange - www.ciee.org
In addition to study and work abroad programs, the CIEE also offers more than 800 volunteer programs. Their web site is comprehensive, and has a "program finder" to help you narrow down the choices. Application information and fee information are also listed. Useful even if you aren't planning on volunteering with them (some of their programs can be pricey), to get a sense of available opportunities.

International Volunteer Programs Association -
www.volunteerinternational.org
Comprehensive listing of volunteer programs. The site is run by volunteer program administrators. Also lists volunteering options that are available for academic credit.

South America Explorers - www.saexplorers.org
Primarily focused on travelers, but also has links to volunteer opportunities in Latin America.

Volunteer Abroad - www.volunteerabroad.com
Part of the GoAbroad network. A great place to start researching the variety and scope of programs available. This is one of the largest directories on the web. It doesn't charge organizations to list, so it attracts listings from smaller organizations and co-ops that wouldn't be able to afford a paid directory. If you can't find it here, it probably doesn't exist.

Volunteering Programs and Organizations

American Friends Service Committee - www.afsc.org
Also known as the Quakers. Has a handful of domestic as well as global (mostly Latin America) volunteer opportunities.

Cross Cultural Solutions - www.crossculturalsolutions.org
The "mini peace corps," operating in 10 different countries. Volunteer opportunities are short-term only (usually 3 weeks) and can be a good way to get your feet wet and see if development work is really for you. Well-organized web site.

Cultural Embrace - www.culturalembrace.com

Private organization offering teaching opportunities in six countries. Not strictly a "volunteer" organization – their focus is on cultural exchange and learning.

Earth Watch - www.earthwatch.org
Organizes "expeditions" where participants get involved in local development and environment issues. Not exactly volunteering, but a fascinating way to see development and conservation in action up close. Pricey.

Global Service Corps - www.globalservicecorps.org
Operates in Thailand and Tanzania. Volunteers stay with a local family. Short-term volunteer programs in health, environment, and education run year-round.

Global Volunteers - www.globalvolunteers.com
Offers short-term placements in 19 different countries. Also structured volunteer teaching opportunities in 12 countries.

i-to-i - www.i-to-i.com
Variety of volunteer placements, including many for teaching English. Excellent web site with lots of behind the scenes information and first-hand accounts.

MBA Enterprise - www.mbaec-cdc.org
The Peace Corps for the MBA crowd. Places recent MBA grads in positions to act as management and business consultants. Currently heavily focused in central Asia and Eastern Europe. Check out for more information on postings, qualifications, and how to apply.

Peace Corps - www.peacecorps.gov
Excellent web site. Packed with information about the Peace Corps, the application process, and what to expect if you/re placed, as well as lots of links and resources in general for overseas work and volunteer opportunities.

Volunteers for Peace - www.vfp.org
Low cost, short term volunteer abroad programs and "work camps." Also provides general volunteer information and link exchanges with other sites.

Volunteer Teach - www.volunteerteach.org
Nonprofit supplying teachers to developing areas – six-month to one-year contracts. Some interesting countries (Namibia, Costa Rica) available for placement.

Visit Vault at **www.vault.com** for insider company profiles, expert advice, career message boards, expert resume reviews, the Vault Job Board and more.

VAULT CAREER LIBRARY   **177**

Recommended Reading for Volunteering

Alternatives to the Peace Corps: A Directory of Third World and U.S. Volunteer Opportunities by Joan Powell

Directory of Work and Study in Developing Countries by Toby Milner

Global Work: InterAction's Guide to Volunteer, Internship and Fellowship Opportunities from Interaction Publications Department

A Handbook for Creating Your Own Internship in International Development by Natalie Foster and Nicole Howell

How to Live Your Dream of Volunteering Abroad, by Joseph Collins Stefano DeZerega and Zahara Heckscher

International Directory of Voluntary Work by Louise Whetter and Victoria Pybus

The Peace Corps and More: 175 Ways to Work, Study and Travel at Home and Abroad by Medea Benjamin and Miya Ridolfo-Sioson

The Post-Soviet Handbook: A Guide to Grassroots Organizations and Internet Resources in the Newly Independent States by M. Holt Ruffin, Joan McCarter, and Richard Upjohn.

Volunteer Vacations: Short Term Adventures That Will Benefit You and Others by Bill McMillon

Study Abroad and Internships Databases and Directories

Action without Borders - www.idealist.org
Internship opportunities with NGOs and development organizations are periodically listed. Most are unpaid.

American Scandinavian Foundation - www.amscan.org
Comprehensive listing for American students looking to study, work or intern abroad in Scandinavian countries. Heavy emphasis on engineering and technology-related placements.

AmidEast - www.amideast.org
Nonprofit site dedicated to fostering international understanding. The focus is on political and cultural issues. Provides listings of internships (many with international non-profits) in the Middle East.

Association for Asian Studies - www.aasianst.org
Information on employment and study opportunities in Asia; lots of scholarly papers and background information on the area. Information on study abroad options and some internships.

CIEE (Center for International Education Exchange) - www.ciee.org
The largest organization devoted to international exchanges, the CIEE offers an extremely wide menu of study abroad, intern, teach and volunteer programs, and has a handy search function to help you narrow down your interest. Lots of background information if you're thinking of studying abroad and not sure where to turn.

Hagshama - www.wzo.org.il
Directory of volunteer and study opportunities in Israel.

Institute of International Education - www.iiepassport.org
Extensive database, searchable for study and work abroad programs. Can't miss with this site. Very user-friendly. Sponsored by the Institute of International Education (administrators of the Fulbright). Visit their sister site, www.iie.org for information on the Institute and other programs and fellowships.

Intern Abroad, College Abroad, Study Abroad - www.internabroad.com, www.collegeabroad.com, www.studyabroad.com.
Three sites part of the large GoAbroad.com series of web sites. Some of the best directories on the web. Helps you sort through the bewildering number of choices.

Women in International Security - www.wiis.org
A good source for international internships from this organization, aimed at women working in foreign policy and overseas government work.

Worldwide Classroom - www.worldwide.edu
A large international consortium of schools. Has information on 10,000 schools in 109 countries. Useful if you're interested in directly enrolling in a school overseas.

Visit Vault at **www.vault.com** for insider company profiles, expert advice, career message boards, expert resume reviews, the Vault Job Board and more.

VAULT CAREER LIBRARY   **179**

Study Abroad and Internships Programs

AISEC - www.aisec.org / www.aisecus.org
The largest student organization in the world, completely student run, arranges for traineeships in more than 85 countries. Check out the web site or the club on campus: www.aiseconline.net or contact your local student club (there are more than 800 chapters).

Brethren Colleges Abroad - www.bcanet.org
Organizes over 100 study abroad programs via 20 academic study centers in 17 countries.

British Universities North America Club (BUNAC) - www.bunac.com
Offer short-term visas for work in casual jobs, such as bartending or au-pairing.

CDS International - www.cdsintl.org
A non-profit organization geared toward international practical training, fellowship, and placement opportunities for young professionals and students. Serves over 50 countries.

Center for International Education Exchange (CIEE) - www.ciee.org
In addition to study abroad programs, CIEE also offers short-term work visas for Australia, New Zealand, Canada, France, Ireland and Germany. Check out their comprehensive web site – click on the "Work Abroad" button.

Center for Study Abroad - www.centerforstudyabroad.com
Private non-profit organization offering study abroad programs (not necessarily for academic credit) in 20 countries. Cheaper than other privately offered programs. The programs are not only for college students but also for working adults, retirees, and other non-students.

German Academic Exchange Service - www.daad.org
Official information about study abroad and internships for Germany

Global Experiences - www.globalexperiences.com
Private company offering combination study and internship programs, including marketing and business-oriented courses. Limited number of countries, and a guaranteed work placement. Pricy.

InterExchange - www.interexchange.org
Non-profit organization offering a variety of work and internship placements for students and non-students, in teaching, au pairing and volunteer work.

International Association for the Exchange of Students for Technical Experience (IASTE) - www.iaste.org
Focused on undergrads in technical fields such as engineering and computing. This program is supported by the U.N. and offers short-term work exchanges and internships in over 80 countries around the world.

International Cooperative Education - www.icemenlo.com
Paid summer internships in a handful of European countries. Language fluency required in specific languages for some positions.

Rotary International - www.rotary.org
Largest scholarship program for U.S. students to study aboard. Visit their web site to learn how to get involved in the organization and apply for the scholarships.

United States State Department - www.state.gov
Series of summer and longer internships, mostly unpaid. Very competitive. Check out the web site for information on internships and fellowships.

Recommended Reading for Study Abroad and Internships

Academic Year Abroad edited by Marie O'Sullivan

Advisory List of International Educational Travel & Exchange Programs from the Council for International Educational Travel

The Au Pair and Nanny's Guide to Working Abroad by Susan Griffith and Sharon Legg

The Back Door Guide to Short Term Job Adventures by Michael Landes

Directory of Overseas Summer Jobs edited by David Woodworth and Ian Collier

Directory of Summer Jobs in Britain edited by David Woodworth

Fellowships in International Affairs: A Guide to Opportunities in the United States and Abroad by the WIIS Institute

The Internship Bible by Mark Oldman and Samer Hamadeh

Peterson's Study Abroad from Peterson's

Peterson's Summer Study Abroad from Peterson's

Visit Vault at **www.vault.com** for insider company profiles, expert advice, career message boards, expert resume reviews, the Vault Job Board and more.

VAULT CAREER LIBRARY   181

Short Term Study Abroad edited by Marie O'Sullivan

The Unofficial Guide to Study Abroad by Ann M. Moore

Work Your Way Around the World by Susan Griffith

Job Hunting Web Sites (General)

Campus Career Center - www.campuscareercenter.com

Career Builder - www.careerbuilder.com

Career Web - www.careerweb.com

Employment Guide - www.employmentguide.com

Job Source Network - www.jobsourcenetwork.com

Job Web - www.jobweb.com

Monster - www.monster.com

MSN Careers - www.msncareers.com

Vault - www.vault.com

Job Sites Focused on Working Abroad

Actions without Borders - www.idealist.org
The largest site for jobs in the nonprofit and development world. Opportunity to post your own resume and browse short-term and long-term consulting positions. Great web site.

Career Journal - www.careerjournal.com
From *The Wall Street Journal*. Working Abroad section with region-specific sites for Europe and Asia.

Escape Artist - www.escapeartist.com.
Slogan: "How to escape from America." Jobs, real estate, and investment advice for moving abroad. An interesting slant on a common topic. Access a wide range of information to help with the overseas job search – job listings, employer directories, foreign newspapers and one of the best sources for jobs overseas. Also lots of information on living, working, and traveling abroad.

Expats Direct - www.expatsdirect.com
U.K.-based. Focused on executive and technical positions.

International Career Employment Center - www.internationaljobs.org
Subscription (fee-based) provider of job listings and a weekly job journal.
Bills itself as the only true international job center on the web – a must for
anyone who is serious about launching an international job search.

Jobs Abroad - www.jobsabroad.com
Billed as a general site and directory, though most of the posts are for
teaching English and casual jobs. Part of the GoAbroad family of directories.

Monster International - http://workabroad.monster.com
Section on the job search behemoth devoted to international jobs, with useful
articles and a Q & A chatroom.

One World - www.oneworld.net
Focus on development and non-profit job postings, some very senior level.

The Riley Guide - www.rileyguide.com
Excellent country-by-country compilation of employment resources on the
Web. One of the best resources for any kind of job hunt on the Internet.

U.S. Agency for International Development - www.usaid.gov
Check out this web site for the official United States government
development agency. Links to careers and internships around the world in a
variety of different streams. Development focused.

USA Jobs - www.usajobs.opm.gov
The official job site of the U.S. government. Check out international jobs in
trade, commerce, and the CIA.

Region-Specific Job Sites

Asia Net - www.asia-net.com
Internships and work placements across Asia. Though jobs are geared toward
foreign job seekers, most positions are for professionals speaking Japanese,
Chinese or Korean, as well as English.

Budget Travel - www.budgettravel.com
Extensive site with Europe information for job seekers, as well as travelers.
Country by country breakdown with local job hunting sites listed as well as
international directories.

LatPro - www.latpro.com
Latin America's professional network. One of the largest job sites aimed at
bilingual professionals for positions in Latin America and North America.

Saludos.com - www.saludos.com
Jobsite for bilingual college graduates for Latin America.

Teaching Abroad Job Sites

Dave's ESL Café - www.eslcafe.com
The original ESL job board and community group. Enormous amount of information as well as great peer-to-peer dialogues on every question and every region imaginable.

Teach Abroad - www.teachabroad.com:
Another web site from the GoAbroad.com network, offers an extensive directory of teaching jobs and positions.

Center for International Education Exchange - www.ciee.org
In addition to study and work abroad programs, the CIEE also offers teaching programs (as a volunteer) for China and Thailand.

ELT Portal - www.tefl.com
Extensive ESL job board. Also offers you the opportunity to post your own resume.

Teachers.net - www.teachers.net
Huge portal for teachers. Lots of classroom resources, lesson plans, game ideas and teaching tips. Good job board.

ESL Focus - www.eslfocus.com
Web "magazine" for ESL teachers. Great resources and a job board with lots of European teaching positions. Chatrooms and message boards help you connect with other teachers and learn about potential schools.

TESOL - www.tesol.org
Web site of the professional association of English teachers. Lots of resources, though geared toward the career ESL teacher rather than new (and unqualified) teachers.

Japan English Teachers Program - www.jetprogramme.org
Official web site of the JET program. Information on how to apply and what to expect.

EPIK Program - www.epik.knue.ac.kr
Official web site of the EPIK Program in Korea.

Jet Alumni - www.jet.org

Jet alumni association. Good source of job posts in Japan, and a good way to network with former JETs.

Recommended Reading for International Jobs

After Latin American Studies: A Guide to Graduate Study and Employment for Latin Americanists by Shirley Kregar and Jorge Nallim

Best CVs and Resumes for International Jobs: Your Passport to the Global Job Market by Ron Krannich and Wendy S. Enelow

The Canadian Guide to Working and Living Overseas by Jean-Marc Hachey

Complete Guide to International Jobs and Careers by Ron and Caryl Krannich

Directory of Jobs and Careers Abroad by Elisabeth Roberts

Directory of Web Sites for International Jobs by Ron and Caryl Krannich

The ELT Guide published by TESOL

Global Resume and CV Guide by Mary Anne Thompson

Great Jobs Abroad by Arthur H. Bell

Great Jobs for Foreign Language Majors by Jule DeGalan and Stephen Lambert

How to Get a Job in Europe: The Insider's Guide by Robert Sanborn and Cheryl Matherly

Inside a US Embassy: How the Foreign Service Works for America edited by Karen Krebsbach

International Job Finder by Daniel Lauber

Make A Mil-Yen: Teaching English in Japan by Don Best

Native Speaker: Teach English and See the World by Elizabeth Reid

Teaching English Abroad: Teach Your Way Around the World by Susan Griffith

Teaching English in Asia: Finding a Job and Doing it Well by Galen Harris Valle

Work Abroad: The Complete Guide to Finding a Job Overseas edited by Clay Hubbs, Susan Griffith and William Nolting

Working in Asia by Nicki Grihault

Networking Resources

American Foreign Service Organization - www.afsa.org,
For more information on what life is like in the Foreign Service and helpful study tips.

An American Abroad - www.anamericanabroad.com
The "hub for Americans abroad," this comprehensive site has a dizzying array of links and resources, including country-specific communities, jobs, politics, government, housing and much much more.

Dave's ESL Café - www.eslcafe.com
Lots of resources for you once you start teaching. Connect with and learn from other teachers.

Expat Exchange - www.expatexchange.com
Huge info portal for living abroad. Lots of practical resources and links, as well as country-specific information and "been there, done that" tales, as well as discussion forums geared toward individual countries.

Expat Forum - www.expatforum.com
Geared toward "expats" and families relocating, this nonetheless has interesting articles and lots of country-specific information.

iAgora - www.iagora.com
In addition to housing, jobs and practical tips, this forum for "internationals" also has numerous clubs and discussion groups covering areas of interest as well as geographic location. At last count, 134 regional and country-based clubs – a great way to connect with other foreigners.

Lonely Planet - www.lp.com
Great virtual community and message boards / chat rooms.

Monster.com - www.monster.com
Chat boards and informative articles for people working abroad, organized by region.

Tales from a Small Planet - www.talesmag.com
Web site for those working with the Foreign Service, includes country reports and "What it's like" reports. Robust chat rooms.

Transitions Abroad - www.transitionsabroad.com
Publishes a bimonthly magazine for those working and studying abroad. Also has a host of information on the free access site. Online magazine devoted to all aspects of living abroad, including program options as well as the practical side of relocation and academic credit. A good first stop for research. Covers study, work, international travel, and living abroad resources.

There are countless country and region-specific virtual communities connecting Americans and other expats with others. Here's a small sampling of region-specific sites.

Amerikanska - www.amerikanska.com
Web site for Americans living in Sweden. Job info, active message boards, and cultural issues.

Americans in France - www.americansinfrance.com
Everything you wanted to know about moving to and living in France.

Association of Americans in Singapore - www.aasingapore.com
Resources for relocating, living, working, and studying in Singapore.

Expatica - www.expatica.com
Resource for expats in Belgium, includes a host of practical advice as well as discussion forums and a job board.

Cultural Issues Resources

Cultural Savvy - www.culturalsavvy.com
A consulting business, but has lots of free resources on their site devoted to cross-cultural business issues and how they can impact business relations.

Executive Planet - www.executiveplanet.com
Country-specific write ups that go into lots of detail on what to expect in all areas of business. Billed as the most comprehensive resource on international business etiquette on the Internet.

Getting Through Customs - www.getcustoms.com
How to do business in 60 countries. Huge resource, countless articles on all different aspects of doing business around the world.

Managing Cultural Differences by Phillip R. Harris, Robert T. Moran

Visit Vault at **www.vault.com** for insider company profiles, expert advice, career message boards, expert resume reviews, the Vault Job Board and more.

VAULT CAREER LIBRARY   **187**

Resources for Practical Issues

Most of the directories and portals described above have comprehensive information on all aspects of relocating and living abroad: visas, plane tickets, accommodation, taxes, emergencies, etc. The following web sites have additional information:

Association of Americans Resident Overseas - www.aaro.org
Volunteer organization representing the interests of Americans living and working abroad.

Embassies in the U.S. - www.embassy.org
This web site has lists of all American-based embassies. Can be useful for information on visas and work authorization in specific countries.

Homestore.com - www.homestore.com
Moving and Relocation calculators to estimate the cost of moving abroad

iAgora - www.iagora.com
Check out their "iHousing" site for short- and long-term housing. Most of the ads are for Europe, though some are for Latin America and Asia. You can also post an ad.

International Student - www.internationalstudent.com
This "one-stop shop" for students going international with information on travel, insurance, medical issues, housing, and applications also offers application and resume writing services. Good discussion boards and chat rooms on a variety of topics.

IRS - www.irs.ustreas.gov
Check out this site for tax information for U.S. citizens living and working abroad.

The SmartStudent Guide to Financial Aid - www.finaid.org
Information on financial aid, including aid available or study and work abroad programs.

The United States State Department - www.state.gov
A first stop for all information for Americans traveling abroad. Lists of embassies and consulates abroad, travel tips and warnings, services, passports, travel publications, as well as excellent background notes and country information

Directory of American Firms Operating in Foreign Countries from Uniworld Press

Directory of International Organizations by Hans-Albrecht Shcraepler

Financial Aid for Study and Training Abroad edited by Gail Ann Schlachter and R. David Weber

Financial Resources for International Study: A Guide for U.S. Nationals edited by Marie O'Sullivan and Sara Steen

Visit Vault at **www.vault.com** for insider company profiles, expert advice, career message boards, expert resume reviews, the Vault Job Board and more.

V/\ULT CAREER LIBRARY 189

About the Author

Sally Christie

Sally Christie's international experience includes working in France, teaching and writing children's books in South Korea, working as a headhunter in China, consulting in Mexico, and marketing for a start-up in Canada. She holds a BA in Anthropology from McGill University and an MBA from Wharton.

Visit Vault at **www.vault.com** for insider company profiles, expert advice, career message boards, expert resume reviews, the Vault Job Board and more.

VAULT CAREER LIBRARY   191

Use the Internet's
MOST TARGETED
job search tools.

Vault Job Board

Target your search by industry, function, and experience level, and find the job openings that you want.

VaultMatch Resume Database

Vault takes match-making to the next level: post your resume and customize your search by industry, function, experience and more. We'll match job listings with your interests and criteria and e-mail them directly to your inbox.